The Treaty of Traverse des Sioux

Other books by William E. Lass:

Stanley J. Morrow: Frontier Photographer, 1956 (co-author).

A History of Steamboating on the Upper Missouri River, 1962.

From the Missouri to the Great Salt Lake:
An Account of Overland Freighting, 1972.

Minnesota: A Bicentennial History (The States and the Nation Series), 1977.

Minnesota's Boundary with Canada: Its Evolution since 1783, 1980.

Minnesota: A History, Second ed., 1998.

Navigating the Missouri: Steamboating on Nature's Highway, 1819–1935, 2008.

The Treaty of Traverse des Sioux

William E. Lass

International Standard Book Number: 978-0-9834668-1-9
Manufactured in the United States of America

Nicollet County Historical Society Press
St. Peter, Minnesota
Publisher

Corporate Graphics
North Mankato, Minnesota
Printer

Contents

Maps & Illustrations

MAPS

ILLUSTRATIONS

Preface

On July 23, 1851, Luke Lea and Alexander Ramsey, co-commissioners of the United States government, and thirty-five chiefs and headman of the Sisseton and Wahpeton bands of the Dakota Indians signed the Treaty of Traverse des Sioux in Minnesota Territory. The treaty was one of the most important events in Minnesota's frontier history. By it and the subsequent Treaty of Mendota with the Mdewakanton and Wahpekute bands of Dakota, the United States acquired most of southern and central Minnesota as well as adjoining portions of Iowa and South Dakota. Hence, the treaties provided the basis for an unprecedented land rush by farmers and townsite promoters into one of the world's richest agricultural regions. The resultant population boom led to Minnesota achieving statehood in 1858.

From the Dakota standpoint, the 1851 treaties marked the transition from their somewhat nomadic hunting and gathering society to reservation life. This was a revolutionary change. During their approximately century and a half of occupying southern Minnesota, the

Dakota had come to regard it as their homeland. But white intrusions, highlighted by the westward advancing farming frontier, posed a major threat to their livelihood by the time Minnesota Territory was formed in 1849.

The purpose of this essay is to present a brief scholarly history of the history of the Treaty of Traverse des Sioux in the context of its time with consideration of both the white and Dakota viewpoints. It is intended to help visitors to the Treaty Site History Center and anyone else interested in Minnesota history gain a better understanding of a very significant occurrence in their past.

It is difficult, if not impossible, to understand Indian treaties without considering land mania in the United States. At the time of the Traverse des Sioux Treaty, Americans generally accepted the doctrine of Manifest Destiny—the belief that they had a God-given right to extend their control over the land and all of its native occupants from ocean to ocean. This attitude, of course, caused advancing frontier people and their political leaders, to regard Indians as a lesser people, who in the parlance of the time were often labeled "savages," which is to say they lacked the characteristics of white society.

The history of the Treaty of Traverse des Sioux, like any other event in the history of the United States, can be approached from local, state and national levels. Some things never have significance beyond their immediate locales. Others, such as the Treaty of Traverse des Sioux, impact the history of their states and provide excellent case studies of national aspirations and policies. With this in mind, I have attempted to place the history of the

Treaty of Traverse des Sioux within the broad framework of state and national history.

This study considers the national and regional background of the Treaty of Traverse des Sioux, the treaty's negotiation, provisions and implementation and its legacy. A verbatim copy of the treaty is included in the appendix.

Several individuals contributed significantly to the production of this history. Ben Leonard, executive director of the Nicollet County Historical Society, encouraged me to undertake the project and managed all production details. Eileen Holz of St. Peter read the manuscript and helped prepare its publication. Eric C. Cronin, a History/Geography major at Gustavus Adolphus College, did the maps. I sincerely thank all of them for their contributions.

William E. Lass
Mankato, Minnesota, May 2011

Treaty Site History Center, 1851 N. Minnesota Ave., St. Peter, Minnesota.

In May 1988, the Nicollet County's Historical Society won a 100-year lease on two acres east of Highway 169 for its new museum. The Nicollet County Historical Society signed a contract, June 6, 1989, for the design of a county museum, by architects Boarman and Associates of Minneapolis, to be located at Traverse des Sioux Park, just north of St. Peter. The Society broke ground for the building, located at the original treaty site, in the spring 1992 and moved from its location at St. Peter's Central Community Center to its new custom-designed facilities in mid-December 1993. The Treaty Site History Center opened Feb. 1, 1994. The Center holds three exhibit halls with both permanent and changing displays, and archives for historical research.

Part 1
Indian Treaties in the United States

By the time the United States began operating under its constitution in 1789, Euro-Americans had experienced nearly three centuries of contact with the native peoples. The leading colonial powers—Great Britain, France and Spain—all made Indian treaties, which were negotiated during sometimes highly ceremonial meetings. The Europeans assumed that each Indian tribe was a sovereign nation. Hence, treaties were negotiated on the premise that the parties were of equal status. But, in reality, the European powers really believed they controlled all land within their realms by the right of discovery. Therefore, they regarded the Indians as the occupiers of the land rather than its legal owners. Although the terms "sell" and "buy" were used in everyday parlance, the Europeans actually meant they were buying Indian occupation rights.[2]

In the course of treating with the natives, the three major European powers, and to a lesser extent, the Netherlands and Sweden, negotiated three types of treaties—peace and friendship, boundary and cession. Under treaties of peace and friendship the whites and Indians agreed to live harmoniously with each other. The treaties of peace and friendship were the most enduring in areas where the fur trade was perpetuated. Under fur trading, which depended on white-Indian partnerships, the natives stayed on their land. But, in the English-speaking colonies that became the original thirteen states, agriculture was the dominant economic activity. Farming and the fur trade were incompatible. Farmers, who wanted to cultivate their own privately owned land, regarded Indian hunting/trading societies as not only remarkably inefficient with respect to their capability of supporting masses of people, but also as a deterrent to white progress. To complicate matters, whites justified their expansion as a way of carrying out the biblical admonishment to till the earth.

Colonial expansion led to Indian land cessions soon after the beginning of the English colonies. For example, Virginia, which was started at Jamestown in 1607, forced a cession treaty on the local Indians within twenty years. Land cessions caused the establishment of formal boundaries separating white and Indian lands. But sometimes boundary treaties delimiting the claims of specific tribes were made prior to cession treaties.

The United States, which was obviously most affected by British tradition based the major assumptions of its Indian policy on colonial precedents. The federal government insisted that it had inherited the right of discovery from whichever European country was the first claimant to a given region of the United States. Thus, like the Europeans, the Americans, while they ostensibly regarded Indian tribes as sovereign nations, really thought that the natives held only occupation rights. Furthermore, the foundation of United States Indian policy was the treaties negotiated with various tribes. Treaties were used to define the original relationship of the United States and any given tribe and any changes in their status had to become the subject of another treaty. Like its European forebears, the United States used a combination of peace and friendship, boundary and cession treaties. In its dealings with the Dakota Indians the federal government first used peace and friendship treaties, then boundary treaties and lastly cession treaties.[3]

Indian relations in the United States were exclusively within the purview of the federal government. The framers of the constitution, well aware of the pitfalls of the colonial system in which each colony had its own Indian policy, gave the federal government the exclusive right to negotiate treaties. On the basis of a constitutional provision and a precedent established in President George Washington's first administration, Indian treaties had to be accepted by a two-thirds vote of members present in the United States Senate. The House of Representatives, while it did not have a voice in approving treaties, was nonetheless involved in any of them requiring appropriations, because the constitution specified that all appropriations bills had to be initiated in the House.[4]

The federal right to deal with Indians meant that Minnesota Territory, like all other territories, could not negotiate with Indians. Therefore, territorial legislatures could do nothing more than request the president and Congress to take a particular action.

Part 2

Dakota Indian Treaties before Traverse des Sioux

When the United States gained its independence from Great Britain by the Treaty of Paris of 1783, its territorial extent included that part of Minnesota east of the Mississippi River. In 1803 when it purchased the Louisiana Territory from France, the United States added that portion of Minnesota west of the Mississippi. When these acquisitions were made the indigenous tribes—the Dakota and the Ojibwe—were working closely with British fur traders and were loyal to Great Britain.[5]

After the Louisiana Purchase, the administration of President Thomas Jefferson tried to weaken British dominance over the Indians of the upper Mississippi region. In 1805 the United States army sent 26-year old Lieutenant Zebulon M. Pike and a party of twenty men from St. Louis to the area near and above the Falls of St. Anthony. Pike's mission included the goals of acquiring from the Dakota Indians sites for a future army post and to warn British traders that they were trespassing on American soil.[6]

When Pike reached present-day Minnesota, he found the Dakota (then called Sioux) controlled most of its west and south and their traditional enemy the Ojibwe (then called Chippewa) dominated the central and northern areas. The Dakota consisted of four bands—the Mdewakanton, Wahpekute, Sisseton and Wahpeton. The principal Mdewakanton villages were along the Mississippi River from about the Falls of St. Anthony downstream to near the later Iowa-Minnesota boundary and on the lower part of the Minnesota River. The much smaller Wahpekute band was concentrated in the Cannon River area west-southwest of the Mdewakanton. The Sissetons and Wahpetons generally lived along the Minnesota River upstream from present-day Chaska with some Sisseton located as far west as Big Stone Lake. Because of their respective locations, the Mdewakanton and Wahpekute were forest dwellers, who depended heavily on hunting deer. But the Sissetons and Wahpeton were prairie cultures with ready access to enormous buffalo herds.[7]

On September 23, 1805, Pike met with a Mdewakanton group on an island near the juncture of the Mississippi and Minnesota (then named the St. Peter's) rivers. He induced two men including Little Crow, a chief and grandfather of the Little Crow of the Dakota War of 1862 fame, to sign a cession treaty. Acting on behalf of the "Sioux Nation" the two men agreed to cede to the United States "for the purpose of establishing military posts, nine miles square at the mouth of the river St. Croix, also from below the confluence of the Mississippi and St. Peters [sic], up the Mississippi, to include the falls of St. Anthony, extending nine miles on each side of the river."[8]

In exchange for these tracts, which included much of later Minneapolis and St. Paul, Pike gave the Mdewakanton some $200 worth of presents, but left the treaty's reimbursement provision blank. In 1808 when the Senate unanimously approved the treaty, it stipulated that the payment would be $2,000 or an equivalent amount of goods.[9]

Although the Pike expedition served notice on the Dakota and British traders that the United States was determined to control the upper Mississippi region, it did not result in an immediate American takeover. After Pike left in 1806, eleven years elapsed before another American army officer entered Minnesota. In the meantime, the Dakota maintained their traditional alliance with the British as Anglo-American relations deteriorated before the War of 1812. Because the British and their Indian allies held most of the upper Mississippi and western Great Lakes regions during the war, some British traders entertained hopes of extending Canada's southern boundary to the Ohio River. But the war-ending Treaty of Ghent, signed on Christmas eve, 1814, was negotiated on the principle of *status quo ante bellum*. The United States and Great Britain were content to revert to their pre-war territorial status. Without any loss of territory, both sides could tell themselves that they had not lost the war. But the war drastically changed the lives of such pro-British Indians as the Dakota. They were left in an Anglophobic United States, which resented their support for the British and was determined to exert its control over them.[10]

Soon after the war the United States launched a diplomatic offensive designed to cause the Dakota and other former British allies to accept American supremacy. In the summer and fall of 1815, federal commissioners negotiated thirteen peace and friendship treaties with Mississippi River regional tribes at Portage des Sioux on the Mississippi's west bank above the mouth of the Missouri. Two of them were with Dakota leaders who were summoned to the treaty site at the present-day town of Portage des Sioux, Missouri.[11]

The Dakota treaties signed at Portage des Sioux were with the "Sioux of the Lakes" and the "Sioux of St. Peter's River," the designations for two small delegations of Mdewakanton leaders. Only a total of eleven Indian men signed the two treaties, which indicates that tribal enthusiasm for them was not widespread. Nonetheless, they achieved the legal objectives of the United States. Pledging themselves to "perpetual peace and friendship" the United States and the Dakota signers agreed that "every injury, or act of hostility, committed by one or either of the contracting parties against the other, shall be mutually forgiven and forgot." The tribesmen further "hereby acknowledge themselves and their aforesaid tribe to be under the protection of the United States, and of no other nation, power, or sovereign, whatsoever."[12]

During the administration of President James Monroe the United States moved to prove to the Indians that it was indeed their sovereign by extending its military frontier to the upper Mississippi. In 1816 the army founded Fort Crawford at Prairie du Chien, Wisconsin, and the next year army Brevet Major Stephen Harriman Long selected the site for a future army post at the confluence of the Mississippi and Minnesota rivers. An army expedition established a cantonment near there in 1819 and began constructing a permanent fort the next year at the Long site. Initially called Fort St. Anthony, the massive stone bastion on a high point looming above the river junction, was re-named to Fort Snelling in 1825.[13]

The War Department, which had jurisdiction over Indian affairs until 1849, used the fort's establishment as an opportunity to establish a Dakota Indian agency. During his tenure (1820–40), agent Lawrence Taliaferro (pronounced Tolliver) maintained his headquarters approximately one-fourth of a mile west of the fort. Taliaferro, who was generally charged with "civilizing" the Dakota had scant resources. The goods due the Dakota by the Pike treaty had been delivered and distributed in 1819, so for their livelihood the Indians had to depend on traditional hunting/gathering and their trade with private American fur traders.[14]

During Taliaferro's administration, the federal government made three treaties that profoundly affected the Dakotas—the Prairie du Chien treaties of 1825 and 1830 and the Treaty of 1837. The 1825 Prairie du Chien Treaty dealt only with tribal boundaries, but the one five years later adjusted boundaries and specified some cessions. The 1837 treaty with the Mdewakanton provided for the cession of their lands east of the Mississippi.

By 1825 rapid American frontier expansion was very evident. In 1787 the government under the Articles of Confederation enacted the Northwest Ordinance, which applied to the area bounded by Pennsylvania on the east, the Ohio River on the south, the Great Lakes on the north and the Mississippi River on the west. Among other things, the ordinance specified a process by which frontier areas could evolve into organized territories and then states. In order to become a territory an area had to have a population of "five thousand free male inhabitants." To make the transition to statehood a territory was normally required to have a population of "sixty thousand free inhabitants."[15]

By 1820 three states—Ohio (1803), Indiana (1816) and Illinois (1818)—had been formed out the Northwest Territory. The remainder of the territory was in Michigan Territory. The new states followed a similar process in being admitted to the union. To promote agriculture and to meet the statehood population requirement, territories prevailed on the federal government to negotiate Indian cession treaties. The territories soon qualified for statehood as white settlers rushed onto the ceded lands. This history indicated that it was just a matter of time until the farming frontier displaced all Indian hunting societies in those regions suitable for cultivation.

In the early 1820s, fur-trading, dominated by the American Fur Company, was the main activity in Michigan Territory. The traders insisted their business, which they claimed was the main agent for introducing American culture into the region, would be improved if intertribal warfare was ended. The government, in response, officially believed that peace would prevail among the tribes if they would agree on tribal boundaries. The Prairie du Chien Treaty involving eight tribes of the upper Mississippi region was negotiated "to promote peace among the tribes"... "and thereby to remove all causes of future difficulty."[16]

Formal, legal boundaries, so familiar to Euro-American individual property owners and political entities, were unknown in Indian cultures. Each tribe regarded its land as a range extending into the zones where it encountered resistance from other tribes. Naturally, such a situation oftentimes led to disputes and wars.

Recognizing Indian tradition, the federal government nonetheless felt obligated to convince the Dakota and other upper Mississippi tribes that they would benefit from mutually acceptable boundaries. This process was started in 1824 when tribal delegations including some Dakota and Ojibwe were escorted to the nation's capital where federal officials broached boundary possibilities with them.[17]

While preparing for the Prairie du Chien council, Taliaferro rendezvoused with a large delegation of Dakota and Ojibwe leaders at Fort Snelling. After some of the Dakota traveled from as far away as Big Stone Lake and some of the Ojibwe from Sandy Lake between Lake Superior and the Mississippi, Taliaferro assembled a party of 385 men. Moving downstream in a flotilla of canoes they joined other tribal delegations at Prairie du Chien.

In terms of sheer numbers the Prairie du Chien conference ranks as one of the greatest assemblages of upper

Mississippi area Indians. Several thousand natives were hosted by federal co-commissioners William Clark and Lewis Cass. Clark, best known for his role in the famous Lewis and Clark expedition, was the superintendent of Indian affairs in St. Louis. Cass, who became a powerful figure in the national Democratic Party, was then serving as governor of Michigan Territory.[18]

After being plied with government-supplied food and liquor during long preliminary dallying, representatives of all four Dakota bands agreed to boundaries separating their claims from those of the Ojibwe on the north and the confederated Sac and Meskwaki (i.e. Fox) on the south. The Dakota-Ojibwe boundary started on the Chippewa River "half a day's march below the falls" (near present-day Osceola, Wisconsin). From there it ran northwestward by a series of streams, lakes and straight connecting lines across the St. Croix and Mississippi rivers to the juncture of the Buffalo and Red rivers near later Georgetown, Minnesota, about fifteen land miles north of present-day Moorhead. The Dakota boundary with the Sac and Meskwaki commenced at the confluence of the Upper Iowa and Mississippi rivers near present-day New Albin, Iowa. It ran west-southwest to the Des Moines River forks (present-day Humboldt, Iowa). From that point it ran directly to mouth of the Rock River, a tributary of the Big Sioux (near present-day Hawarden, Iowa). It then followed the southward flowing Big Sioux to its juncture with the Missouri near later Sioux City, Iowa.[19]

The eastern starting points of the southern and northern Dakota boundaries were the basis for drawing the eastern Dakota boundary. The treaty specified that the line would commence on the east side of the Mississippi directly opposite the mouth of the Upper Iowa. With the intention of assuring the Dakota control of the river bluffs, the boundary was run northward to the mouth of the Black River (about 15 miles northwest of present-day La Crosse, Wisconsin) by keeping two to three miles east of the river. From the Black-Mississippi confluence the boundary passed up the Black River to a point some ten miles north of later Neillsville, Wisconsin. From there it lay westerly to the beginning point of the Dakota-Ojibwe boundary.

Despite the government's naive premise that the tribal boundaries would bring peace to the tribes, they never served that purpose. Unfortified demarcations were hardly a deterrent to rival warriors. But they did have one practical use that the government never advanced as a rationale for them. They legally defined tribal lands and thus became the basis for later cession treaties.

Within a short time federal officials acknowledged that warfare was continuing between the Dakota and Sac and Meskwaki. Their solution was to negotiate modifications to the 1825 treaty at Prairie du Chien in 1830. Because of concern about the government's relationship with other tribes, they also wanted Dakota cessions west of the Des Moines River.

In the second Treaty of Prairie du Chien, co-commissioners William Clark and army Colonel Willoughby Morgan, conferred with representatives of the four Dakota bands as well as delegations from the Sac and

Meskwaki and Otoe. In the treaty signed on July 15, 1830, the Dakota and the Sac and Meskwaki agreed to greatly modify the 1825 boundary. Each side ceded to the United States a twenty-mile wide strip flanking their 1825 boundary line from the mouth of the Upper Iowa about 200 miles southwestwardly to the Des Moines River. The forty-mile wide ceded tract, subsequently identified as the "Neutral Ground" was to serve at a buffer between the Dakota and the Sac and Meskwaki.[20]

West of the Des Moines River the boundary was abolished by massive Dakota and Sac and Meskwaki cessions. The tribes relinquished all their claims south of a land line that ran around the northern end of the drainage areas of the Floyd and Little Sioux rivers and a water line formed by Rock River and its easternmost tributary.

The cessions east and west of the Des Moines affected two parts of present-day Minnesota. The northern boundary of the "Neutral Ground," which became the new southern boundary for the Dakota, started on the Mississippi's west bank in the northeast corner of Houston County. From there it ran southwesterly to the later Minnesota-Iowa boundary about twelve miles due south of Preston, Minnesota. West of the Des Moines the line drawn round the northernmost sources of the Floyd and Little Sioux included a triangular-shaped tract in later Nobles and Jackson counties, Minnesota.

Other than adjusting their southern boundary line, the Dakota in the 1830 Prairie du Chien Treaty, ceded about 500 square miles on the Minnesota side of Lake Pepin. The fifteen-mile deep tract paralleled the Mississippi for thirty-two miles from present-day Red Wing to below Wabasha. According to the treaty, this cession was made at the request of the Dakota representatives who wanted to benefit the mixed-bloods living among them. Mixed-bloods, the progeny of white traders and Indian women, were identified in the treaty by their then common label as "half breeds." By 1830 these people were numerous enough to constitute a politically significant faction in the Dakota bands. The treaty's wording leaves the impression that the chiefs and headmen made the mixed-blood cession out of the goodness of their heart. But, it is likely they were persuaded by traders, who often had kinship ties to both Indians and mixed-bloods. The transfer of land from the Dakota bands to the mixed-bloods potentially would make it easier for traders and other white interests to acquire it.[21]

The condition of the easternmost Dakota worsened soon after the second Prairie du Chien Treaty. The declining fur trade accompanied by the ravages of a smallpox outbreak caused Taliaferro to conclude that the Mdewakanton needed the income from a land cession. He was able to arrange such a treaty soon after Wisconsin Territory was formed in 1836. The massive new territory encompassed all of present-day Wisconsin , Iowa and Minnesota and those parts of North Dakota and South Dakota east of the Missouri and White Earth rivers. Henry Dodge, its first governor and ex-officio superintendent of Indian affairs, eagerly sought Indian land cessions east of the Mississippi. With Dodge's blessing, Taliaferro lead a delegation of twenty-six Mdewakanton chiefs and headmen to Washington, D.C., in the summer of 1837.[22]

The Mdewakanton leaders were told they were being taken to Washington to arrange another peace settlement with the Sac and Meskwaki. But when representatives of those tribes did not appear, Secretary of War Joel E. Poinsett, representing the United States, convinced the Mdewakanton, in a treaty signed September 29, to cede their lands east of the Mississippi as well as the islands in the river. In the later State of Minnesota this was the tract between the Mississippi and St. Croix rivers and south of the Dakota-Ojibwe boundary line.[23]

For its part, the United States agreed to pay the Mdewakanton $300,000, which would be invested by the government. From that investment the Indians would receive "annually, forever, an income of not less than five per cent." The relatives and friends of the Mdewakanton signers who had "not less than one quarter of Sioux blood" were to be paid $110,000. Additionally, the government agreed to pay the "just debts" (i.e. money owed traders) of the Mdewakanton to the extent of $90,000. Annually for twenty years, the Mdewakanton were to receive $5,500 worth of provisions to be delivered at government expense and $8,250 worth "of medicines, agricultural implements and stock and for the support of a physician, farmers, and blacksmiths, and for other beneficial objects."

Three months before the Mdewakanton signed the Washington treaty, Henry Dodge, in a Fort Snelling treaty, persuaded the Ojibwe to cede some land north of the Dakota-Ojibwe boundary. In later Minnesota this lay between the Mississippi and St. Croix rivers and south of an almost due east-west line running from the mouth of the Crow Wing River to the St. Croix River.[24]

In 1838 the Dakota and Ojibwe treaties were approved by the Senate and proclaimed to be in effect by President Martin Van Buren. Their combined effect was to add some five thousand square miles of land between the Mississippi and the St. Croix to the federal public domain.

Part 3
Minnesota's Quest for Dakota Lands

Rapid white frontier expansion and the accompanying decline in Indian power that contributed to the 1837 treaties affecting Minnesota were accelerated in the 1840s. With Manifest Destiny at a fever pitch, the United States annexed Texas (1845), obtained the Pacific Northwest by resolving a boundary dispute with Great Britain (1846) and acquired California and the southwest as a result of the Mexican-American War (1848). These moves, which made the United States a transcontinental power, had grave implications for the native inhabitants. Belief in Manifest Destiny justified internal expansion against Indians as well as external expansion against foreign governments.[25]

During this burst of national expansion significant changes were made in the upper Mississippi region. In 1838 Congress created Iowa Territory, which included the present state as well as those parts of Minnesota, North Dakota and South Dakota west of the Mississippi, south of the Canadian boundary and east of the Missouri and White Earth rivers. The same act made the Mississippi the western boundary of Wisconsin Territory.[26]

Wisconsin Territory's political leaders generally assumed their future state would have the same extent as the territory. The Northwest Ordinance had specified that not more than five states would be created out of the Northwest Territory. With Michigan statehood (1837) four had been formed, so the ordinance seemingly dictated that Wisconsin would have to extend westward to the Mississippi and a direct line from its northernmost source to the international boundary.[27]

Most of Wisconsin Territory's first settlers were lead miners or farmers in the approximate southernmost quarter of the later state. But there was also a trickle of emigrants into the southernmost part of the delta-shaped tract acquired by the 1837 Dakota and Ojibwe treaties. This frontier section, which was quite accessible by steamboats, was particularly appealing to New England lumbermen. Attracted by the great stands of white pine, some Maine lumberman built a sawmill at Marine on St. Croix in 1839. Other mills were soon operating upstream at Stillwater and St. Croix Falls. By the mid-1840s Stillwater was the leading St. Croix valley settlement. Meanwhile, St. Paul (originally named Pig's Eye) had been founded as the practical head of Mississippi River steamboating. About ten miles upstream from St. Paul, developers started St. Anthony at the site of the Falls of St. Anthony.[28]

While this movement was occurring, Iowa was admitted to statehood in 1846 and Wisconsin applied for statehood the same year. As Wisconsin went through the statehood process Stillwaterites and St. Paulites campaigned to be left out of the future state. Separated by about three hundred miles of unoccupied country from Madison, Wisconsin's capital, they had no affinity for Wisconsin and wanted to become the key cities in a new state. With the considerable help of Congress, they succeeded. When Wisconsin became a state on May 29, 1848, its western boundary was formed by the Mississippi and St. Croix rivers and a direct line from the falls of the St. Louis River (southwest of Duluth) to the St. Croix. Northern congressmen, who were then engaged in the power struggle between free and slave states, wanted to limit Wisconsin's size. They reasoned that if Wisconsin was made considerably smaller than its seeming Northwest Ordinance destiny, they would create the basis for a new northern state to its northwest. Flaunting the desires of Wisconsin expansionists, who wanted a western boundary of the Mississippi and direct line to Canada, Congress decided it had the authority to change the terms of the Northwest Ordinance.[29]

Although the roughly one thousand people living west of the St. Croix generally wanted to be excluded from Wisconsin, they soon realized that Wisconsin statehood left them in a political no-man's land. Once they were removed from Wisconsin Territory's laws, all legal transactions were jeopardized. Consequently, area leaders convened a political conclave—the Stillwater Convention—to select a delegate from the Minnesota area to represent it in Congress. Although Henry H. Sibley, the chosen delegate, was later elected to the delegacy from the presumed still-existent Wisconsin Territory, the main effect of his seating in Congress was to promote the creation of Minnesota Territory.[30]

Sibley, seated in the House of Representatives, worked closely with Stephen Douglas of Illinois. Douglas, a champion of western expansion, promoted Minnesota's interests to the point of grossly exaggerating that the area had a population of at least 8,000 to 10,000. With this assurance, Congress approved the creation of Minnesota Territory on March 3, 1849, only a day before the outgoing Democratic President James K. Polk was to be replaced by Zachary Taylor, a Whig. Congressional Whigs cooperated with the Democrats in creating Minnesota Territory with the understanding that Taylor would select the territory's executive and judicial officials.[31]

Taylor subsequently appointed Alexander Ramsey, who had served in the House of Representatives as a Whig from Pennsylvania, territorial governor. Ramsey, who was only thirty-four years old, proved to be a good choice for Minnesota's purposes. Like most of the people in the territory he was an expansionist. He also worked effectively with Democrats, who then dominated Minnesota politics. As soon as Ramsey arrived in St. Paul, he and Sibley began contemplating a major land cession by the Dakota Indians. They agreed that Minnesota's future lay in agriculture and the most productive lands were in the valleys of the Mississippi and Minnesota rivers and adjacent areas.

In what amounted to a "state of the territory" message, Ramsey outlined Minnesota's status and prospects to the territorial legislature. He emphasized that the vast territory of about 166,000 square miles (nearly twice as large as the later state) was undeveloped. Bounded by Wisconsin on the east, Iowa and the Missouri River on the south, the Missouri and White Earth rivers on the west and Canada on the north, the territory had only 4,535 residents according to a census taken in the summer of 1849. Most of them lived in the St. Paul-Stillwater area in the triangle formed by the Mississippi and St. Croix rivers. Although this region had some agriculture, its economy depended mainly on lumbering and steamboating. Ramsey reminded the legislators that the estimated 25,000 Indians in the territory still controlled about 97 per cent of the land. If Minnesota was to grow and prosper, he warned, it had to attract thousands of settlers. Minnesota's greatest asset, he asserted, was the prime agricultural lands west of the Mississippi held by the Dakota Indians. He insisted they had to be acquired to assure Minnesota's future prosperity.[32]

Ramsey was so anxious to acquire the Suland, as the Dakota lands came to be known in the frontier press, that he tried to assemble a conclave with Dakota leaders in the fall of 1849. The effort failed miserably, because the Indians, acting on the advice of fur traders, refused to cooperate with unknown government officials.[33]

The fur trade in Minnesota was then dominated by Pierre Chouteau, Jr., and Company of St. Louis, the successor of the American Fur Company. Its principal Minnesota agent was Henry H. Sibley, who had established his headquarters at Mendota, south across the Minnesota River from Fort Snelling, in 1834.[34]

During Sibley's time as the Mendota factor, the fur trade declined sharply. The virtual disappearance of beaver, the drastic reduction of large grazing animals such as buffalo and elk, the Panic of 1837 and its depressive aftermath, competition from independent traders after the 1837 cession treaties, and the granting of annuities to the Mdewakanton all contributed to the trade's bad fortunes. As the trade ebbed, Sibley and his traders continued to extend credit in the form of goods to the Dakota. While Dakotas were unable to repay their obligations with furs, the traders maintained records of this indebtedness. As the Indian debts accrued, the traders recognized that their only real chance of recouping their losses would be when the Dakota sold their lands.

Sibley and his associates were eager for a Dakota cession. But they wanted it to occur under circumstances favorable to them. They realized that the Dakota leaders depended on them for legal advice and guidance in relations with the federal government. The traders' influence was so pervasive that Sibley was able to boast "the Indians are all prepared to make a treaty when we tell them to do so, and such an one as I may dictate."[35]

After Ramsey's failed treaty effort, agitation for acquisition of the Suland became the popular topic of the day. The campaign was stimulated by newspaper editors, townsite promoters and land seekers, all of whom promoted Minnesota. To them a Dakota cession was vital to assure that Minnesota would benefit from an unprecedented surge of white westward movement. The United States was in the midst of a spectacular population boom. The census of 1830 showed the nation had 12,866,020 residents including 2,009,043 slaves but the 1850 count was 23,191,876 including 3,204,313 slaves.[36]

When Minnesota Territory was created, national attention was focused on California. The discovery of gold in the foothills of the Sierra Nevada Mountains sparked the California gold rush in 1849. In that year an estimated 25,000 people moved west to California via overland trails. The next year the migration amounted to 44,000. Minnesota, meanwhile, was suffering from its reputation as a cold, inhospitable land unfit for habitation. Minnesota's promoters realized that to compete with California they had to extol their territory as the next great farming frontier. They could not do this as long as the Dakota controlled the most productive lands.[37]

Most of the agitation for acquisition of the Suland emanated from St. Paul, the territorial capital. Situated across the Mississippi from the Dakota lands, St. Paul was the logical base for Minnesota's expansionists. In addition to being the seat of government it was the principal steamboat port on the upper Mississippi. In the railroad-less territory steamboats were the fastest and most efficient way of moving people and freight.

To spur public interest and congressional action in acquiring the Suland, St. Paul's businessmen organized four Minnesota River steamboat excursions in the summer of 1850. On June 28, Captain Daniel Able navigated the *Anthony Wayne* on an all-day round-trip voyage to the

Little Rapids of the Minnesota River near later Chaska. This excursion was a rousing success. The steamer was crammed with some 300 passengers including a small band. Without doubt, the most important passenger was James M. Goodhue, editor of the *Minnesota Pioneer*, St. Paul's and Minnesota's first newspaper. Although the passengers caught only a glimpse of a tiny portion of the Suland, it was enough for Goodhue to laud the "rich valley"..."along which the covetous eye of the white man has long gazed with prying curiosity."[39]

The *Anthony Wayne's* trip prompted a rival captain to organize another excursion on the *Nominee*, a regular packet in the St. Louis-St. Paul trade. On July 13 Captain Orren Smith navigated the boat just high enough to claim bragging rights for having reached the highest point of steamboat navigation on the Minnesota River. He turned the boat around about three miles above the Little Rapids, but not before advertising his achievement with a painted sign placed on shore.[40]

With the aim of probing farther up the valley, some St. Paulites organized a second voyage by the *Anthony Wayne*. On this trip the boat was navigated past Traverse des Sioux, then the site of a mission station operated by the American Board of Commissioners for Foreign Missions, to a point two to three miles downstream (i.e. north) from later Mankato.

The season's last voyage proved to be the most successful. In a five-day round-trip voyage Captain Martin K. Harris navigated the *Yankee*, beyond the mouth of the Blue Earth (present-day Mankato) to near the later village of Judson. Harris, determined to surpass the *Wayne's* high point, started out with 200 bushels of coal and a cargo hold full of dry wood for fuel. As he knew, the prior excursion boats had been delayed by the need to make frequent wood-gathering stops. Thus prepared, the excursionists including men, women and children as well as part of the Fort Snelling band and Goodhue, got underway on July 22. Once Harris reached the sign marking the end of the *Wayne's* ascent, he found the snag-infested sharp bend that had forced it to turn about. But, responding to the urgings of his enthusiastic passengers, some of whom wanted to go all the way to Big Stone Lake, he managed to push the boat through. But clouds of mosquitoes, scrounging for wood when the temperature soared to 104 and concern about the children's health, soon caused him to turn around.[41]

The steamboat excursions were important advertising for the attractiveness of the Suland. Word-of-mouth stories from participants as well as Goodhue's coverage stimulated public enthusiasm for the fertile lands. In providing his readers a word picture of the land, Goodhue wrote: "What unrivalled beauty of landscape, now we pass through dense forests, now through prairie, and anon stretches away a vast savanna of tall prairie grass, thousands of acres in extent, with a vista of high prairie opening in the distance between forests, as far as the sight can extend."[42] Furthermore, the voyages proved the practicability of steamboat navigation on the Minnesota. Consequently, later settlers would be assured of steamboat service, which was much faster and cheaper than overland wagon transportation. Steamboating would also help stimulate commercial agriculture, because quantities of wheat, the frontier's leading cash crop, could be exported to distant markets.

While Minnesota's promoters enthused about their bright future, the condition of many Dakotas worsened. In 1846 a large buffalo herd moved southeastward into the Minnesota River valley between Big Stone Lake and the Lac qui Parle River. This fortuitous event briefly revived the fortunes of the resident Sissetons. But their short trade revival was ruined by the cold, snowy winter of 1849–50, which was preceded by ruinous prairie fires that blackened the plains. Lack of forage caused the buffalo herd to migrate far westward toward the Missouri River. Without access to the animals, the Sissetons were entirely dependent on their meager trade with Sibley's traders. The results were calamitous. Martin McLeod, the Lac qui Parle post trader, estimated that a third of the Sissetons in the vicinity of his station starved to death over the winter. McLeod believed their only salvation was government support in exchange for ceding their lands. Consequently, part of the rationale for a cession treaty was that it would be a humane action.[43]

Meanwhile, Sibley who was well-informed about Minnesota developments, worked in Washington to arrange Dakota treaty negotiations that would benefit the territory, the traders and ostensibly the Dakota. He wanted congressional appropriations ample enough to acquire the Suland, provide for the future of the Dakotas and reimburse himself and his traders. To accomplish these aims, he needed sympathetic treaty commissioners. Federal government relations with Indians were changed somewhat by the creation of the Interior Department in 1849. The law authorizing the department also transferred to it from the War Department jurisdiction over Indian affairs. This made the commissioner of Indian affairs, who headed the Bureau of Indian Affairs, a subordinate of the secretary of the interior. Thus, in his lobbying efforts, Sibley had to influence the secretary of the interior, the commissioner of Indian affairs and members of Congress, who would have to approve appropriations for Indian land cessions.[44]

All the involved parties agreed that two commissioners would be named to treat with the Dakota and that Ramsey, because of his position as ex-officio superintendent of Indian affairs for Minnesota Territory, would be one of them. Sibley, who could count on Ramsey's support, also wanted a sympathetic co-commissioner. Aside from his public role in representing Minnesota Territory, Sibley had a personal interest in the outcome of the treaties. He and his group of traders who were associated with Pierre Chouteau, Jr., and Company of St. Louis, the successor of John Jacob Astor's American Fur Company, saw Dakota treaties as a marvelous opportunity to recoup their trading losses.[45]

However, Sibley and his associates were leery of the Ewing brothers, longtime Indian traders based in Fort Wayne, Indiana. In 1850 William G. and George W. Ewing, because of their interest in the removal of Winnebago Indians from northeastern Iowa to Long Prairie,

Minnesota Territory, established a foothold in Minnesota's Indian business. Sibley naturally feared the Ewings wanted to extend their trade to the Dakota by influencing the outcome of the pending treaties. For a time it appeared that the Interior Department would select an Indiana man allied with the Ewing brothers to be Ramsey's co-commissioner. But, probably because of some artful lobbying by Sibley, Congress barred this attempt by stipulating in its Indian appropriations act that the second commissioner had to be an employee of the Bureau of Indian Affairs.

Sibley, who had a unique talent for political schmoozing benefitted from his friendship with Luke Lea, the commissioner of Indian affairs. During the winter of 1850–51 Sibley and his wife Sarah stayed in the same Washington rooming house as Lea. As a result of their conversations about the pending Dakota treaty, Lea agreed to be the co-commissioner. His formal naming by Secretary of the Interior Alexander H.H. Stuart evidently pleased everyone but the Ewings. Lea, who was predisposed to favor Sibley's traders, satisfied the congressional requirement that the second commissioner had to be a Bureau of Indian Affairs employee and his Mississippi background helped sooth certain Southern anxieties about a major Indian land cession in a northern area.[46]

Acting on the advice of Sibley and his traders, Lea and Ramsey decided to negotiate two treaties with the Dakota rather than confront a possibly united, recalcitrant tribe in a single conclave. The commissioners chose to treat with Sisseton and Wahpeton leaders first at Traverse des Sioux and then meet with the Mdewakanton and Wahpekute at Mendota. Because of their relative locations along the Minnesota River, the Sisseton and Wahpeton were then often called the upper Sioux and the Mdewakanton and Wahpekute the lower Sioux. The traders believed that the upper Sioux, who lacked experience in making a cession treaty and who were in dire economic straits, would be more receptive to the government's offer than the lower Sioux. Once they agreed to a treaty it could be used as a model to be imposed on the lower Sioux. Lea and Ramsey had decided to follow this divide and conquer strategy before Lea, who traveled on the steamboat *Excelsior*, reached St. Paul on June 27, 1851.[47]

Traverse des Sioux, the selected meeting point with the upper Sioux, had advantages possessed by no other site. As the traditional crossing of the Minnesota River it was well known to the Sisseton and Wahpeton, who were alerted to the impending treaty negotiations by runners sent out by Sibley's traders. Although it was near the eastern edge of the upper Sioux range, Traverse des Sioux was a symbolic halfway point between tribal villages and St. Paul. Because the commissioners wanted to transport supplies sufficient enough to sustain their party and conceivably hundreds of Indians for some time they wanted to meet at a place that was an attained steamboat destination. Lastly, Traverse des Sioux had some minimal accommodations in the form of two abandoned log buildings previously used by trader Louis Provencalle, one of Sibley's associates.

Part 4

Treaty of Traverse des Sioux Negotiations

Anxious to begin negotiating with the Sissetons and Wahpetons, Lea and Ramsey promptly organized their party after Lea's arrival in St. Paul. On June 28 the *Excelsior* was steamed to Mendota and Fort Snelling. Ramsey came aboard the next morning. The commissioners originally planned to be accompanied by a detachment of troops from Fort Snelling, which would serve as their security guard. But when the soldiers were tardy in reaching the landing, Lea and Ramsey decided to leave without them. The steamer was crammed with passengers, supplies, gifts to be distributed at the treaty's signing and cattle. Other than the commissioners, the passengers included their assistants, newspaper man James M. Goodhue and Frank Blackwell Mayer, a young Baltimore, Maryland, artist. Mayer, traveling at his own expense, had requested and been granted Ramsey's permission to attend the treaty negotiations. To Mayer this was a golden opportunity to illustrate part of the epic story of the white man's advance and the end of a free-roaming Indian society.[48]

Because of unusually high water the *Excelsior* made a quick run to Traverse des Sioux. After one dawn-to-dusk day it was within about fifteen miles of its destination. The next morning, June 30, after steaming for a few hours the boat was tied up on a river bend about half a mile northeast of the American Board mission.

The *Excelsior* did not have enough capacity to carry all the cattle needed for subsistence during the negotiations. On or about June 20 a drove of cattle was started for Traverse des Sioux from Mendota. This move had the unfortunate result of causing Shakopee, a Mdewakanton chief, and many of his people to follow in the wake of the herd. The presence of these uninvited guests at the treaty site contributed to possible food shortages.[49]

Goodhue was awed by the remoteness of Traverse des Sioux. He observed that it was merely "a feeble outpost far in the savage wilderness, occupied by the missionary families and a trader or two but with a temporary population of about thirty persons [i.e. the whites in the treaty party]. . . ."[50] The mission station, which stood in open country near some oak trees on the first level above the river and facing it, was composed of three white framed buildings—the chapel-school and the houses of missionary Robert Hopkins and his blacksmith-farmer assistant Alexander G. Huggins and their families. Mixed-blood trader Alexander D. Graham's house and store stood at the boat landing about one-fourth of a mile north of the mission buildings. About one-third of a mile northwest of the mission on the second level above the river were two abandoned log buildings that had once been used by trader Louis Provencalle. These were located on the north side of a little gully that ran down to the river. Just south of the gully there was a small cemetery, started and maintained by former French-speaking traders, bordered by a white picket fence. The Lac Qui Parle trail, the southernmost segment of the route connecting Mendota and the Red River valley, ran on the river side of the Provencalle structures.[51]

The treaty party pitched its seven tents next to the old Provencalle buildings, which were appropriated for storage and mess hall facilities. Veteran trader Alexis Bailly, who had been appointed commissary chief, supervised camp logistics.[52]

When they landed, Lea and Ramsey expected there would be hundreds of Sissetons and Wahpetons on hand and that they would be able to immediately start negotiating. Instead, they found only the thirty to forty lodges of the Sisseton who lived at Traverse des Sioux. The arrival of the various Sisseton and Wahpeton groups was delayed by an uncommonly rainy, late season. Torrential spring and early summer downpours at Traverse des Sioux delayed corn planting until late June. The year before the corn was shoulder-high and tasseling by mid-July. The deluges were widespread throughout a broad region. They caused creeks and otherwise dry coulees to flood, which forced the treaty-bound Sisseton and Wahpeton to wait until the waters receded.

Under the circumstances, Lea and Ramsey had no choice other than to wait until large groups arrived. As they well knew, Indian societies did not have a concept

Sisseton Lodges at Traverse des Sioux, 1851
by Frank Blackwell Mayer (1827–1899), Graphite on paper, 1851. From the collection of the Newberry Library, Chicago, Illinois.

of representative government. Chiefs, who usually inherited their positions from their fathers, were not despots. Tribal mores dictated that they had to consult with their people on all matters. Consequently, operating without the practice of majority rule, they felt obliged to be influenced by minority opinions. As a result, chiefs preferred that all of their people be present at treaty negotiations. These practices caused problems for Lea and Ramsey. They were well aware that the chiefs desired that all of their people including women and children be present. But they were also disposed to say that a majority would suffice. Their concern about recognizing a representative group had supply implications, because the commissioners provided all the food for the assembled Indians.

Finally on July 18, after nearly three weeks of frustrating delays, Lea and Ramsey decided to open negotiations. During the long wait the daily tedium of camp life reigned. The treaty officials and white spectators were plagued by continuing rains, pesky insects and a monotonous diet. Goodhue, somewhat dramatically, described one of the nighttime thunder storms as "the wind flapping and swaying the tents over, like sail-boats in a tempest—the rain streaming, as if the gates of heaven had been stove in and the waste-gates of the clouds hoisted; the lightning blazing with glare enough to burst the eyeballs, red-hot bolts seeming to run everywhere like hungry demons; it glowed as if hell was uncapped, and the terrible thunderbolts pulsated upon the ground with a force like the jarring blows or an earthquake—the water poured in sheets through the tents and wigwams. . . ."[53] The frequent rains assured a surplus of both buffalo gnats (i.e. black flies) and mosquitoes. Burning putrid smudge pots provided the most effective relief from the pests. The gnats, active all day, were relieved by the mosquitoes who worked the dusk and night shifts. There was no difference in the meals except for the time of day. They invariably featured three items—boiled beef from freshly killed cattle, soup made from the beef broth and hardtack.[54]

The white treaty party welcomed any diversion that helped break up their days. Sometimes this was provided by lacrosse games, which were colorful spectacles. As played by the Dakota and other Indians, the rules of the game were very loose. For example, team sizes were not limited to evenly matched small squads. On one occasion 250 Indian men participated. Another game featured only women and girls and yet another matched some of Shakopee's men against some Sissetons and Wahpetons. Invariably, many Indian and white spectators gambled on the outcome by putting up various prizes.[55]

The arrival of Indian groups was usually done with great fanfare. The advancing horse-mounted warriors with their women and children in tow presented themselves to the commissioners with ceremonial approaches featuring mock military maneuvers such as a cavalry charge.

Other than the entertainment provided by the Dakotas, the Traverse des Sioux experience featured the tragic drowning of missionary Robert Hopkins and the wedding of Nancy Winona McClure. On the morning of

July 4, Hopkins, who could not swim went bathing in the river. He stepped into a hole, disappeared beneath the surface and drowned. His body was recovered, but his death cast a pall over the proceedings. Lea and Ramsey had planned a Fourth of July celebration with the Dakotas featuring Indian music, the reading of the Declaration of Independence and a feast. But Hopkins's demise caused them to cancel it.[56]

The wedding of McClure and David Faribault on July 11 was one of the main highlights of the treaty preliminaries. Much of its fascination to the visiting whites was that it symbolized noteworthy social aspects of frontier culture. McClure, the fourteen-year old mixed-blood daughter of Fort Snelling army lieutenant James McClure and a Dakota woman had been cared for and educated at Traverse des Sioux by the Huggins family. Even before the wedding she had attracted the attention of Goodhue and other visitors because of her striking beauty and literacy. Faribault, the mixed-blood son of the famous French-Canadian trader Jean Baptiste Faribault, was portrayed by Goodhue as "a large, handsome man about 30 years old." Alexis Bailly, in his capacity of a justice of the peace, presided over the marriage ceremony.

Lea, who seems to have been unable to pass up an opportunity to pontificate, used the occasion to promote the pending treaty negotiations. After the wedding all guests attended a dinner replete with toasts and speeches. Responding to a toast proffered by trader Joseph La Framboise, Lea, speaking through La Framboise as interpreter, identified himself as "the head of that department which has under its care all the red children of our Great Father." He assured the Dakota that the Great Father (President Millard Fillmore) esteemed the Dakota so much that he had sent Lea as his personal representative from distant Washington to treat with them. Lea explained that the Great Father would pay a fair price for the Dakota land, most of which could be spared by the tribe. He foresaw a "good treaty" that "will ameliorate the condition of the red man to a degree gratifying to the philanthropist and the Christian, will likewise open a magnificent country to the improvements and refinements of civilized life, dotting the banks of this beautiful river before us with thriving towns and bustling cities, and these broad and fertile plains with cultivated fields, glowing firesides, and happy homes."[57]

As the days passed and more and more Sissetons and Wahpetons drifted in, rumors would sweep through the encampment that negotiations were about to start. But the commissioners and the chiefs would decide to wait for yet more people. The transformation of Traverse des Sioux from an outpost into the congregation of perhaps the greatest single Dakota assemblage in Minnesota's history was a spectacle. As early as July 5, when about a thousand Dakota were encamped there, Goodhue reported hastily constructed teepees were "scattered everywhere along the ridges of prairie. ..."[58] and around them hundreds of women and children played during the day. Numerous animals further enlivened the encampment. Dogs cavorted or lounged around the teepees. Indian ponies were tethered on the adjacent grassland so each could graze in a small circular area. Nearby the cattle herd, which was being reduced as daily butchering was done, grazed on the prairie.

During the morning of July 18, just after the arrival of the last group that they expected to be involved in the negotiations, Lea and Ramsey proclaimed that negotiations would commence immediately. They and the Dakota leaders met on the north side of the little gully in what William G. Le Duc called a "council-house". The structure, erected days before under the supervision of Alexis Bailly, in Le Duc's words "consists of a number of benches placed in front of a rude platform and desk of rough boards, which is occupied by the commission when in council, the whole shaded by an arbor of poles covered with boughs of trees." Artist Frank Blackwell Mayer wrote that the arbor was "formed of green boughs laid upon a frame work of young trees.... At one end on a raised platform was placed a table behind which sat the commissioners [,] the American flag was hoisted behind them a few feet from the arbor.... In a semicircle in front of the commission, the chiefs were seated on benches...."[59]

Lea and Ramsey opened their July 18 meeting and all subsequent sessions with the ceremonial passing of a peace pipe among themselves and the chiefs. In his opening remarks Ramsey emphasized that the "Great Father," who had heard of the distressed condition of the Dakotas, had ordered himself and Lea "to see if something cannot be done for your improvement and real welfare." Ramsey reminded the chiefs that their vast

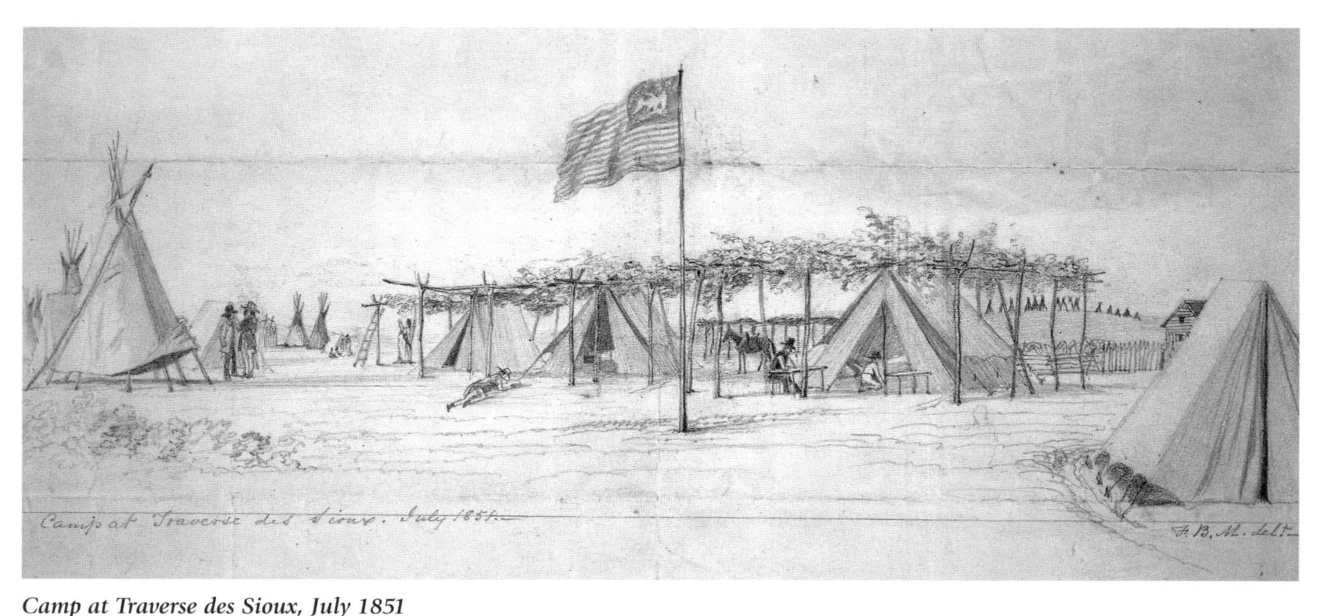

Camp at Traverse des Sioux, July 1851
by Frank Blackwell Mayer (1827–1899), Graphite on paper, 1851. From the collection of the Minnesota Historical Society.

Frank B. Mayer, a Baltimore artist, journeyed to Traverse des Sioux and Mendota on the Minnesota frontier in 1851 to record meetings between United States officials and Indian tribes who were ceding title to much of Southern Minnesota and portions of Iowa and Dakota. Mayer made extensive journal entries and countless sketches while on his travels in Minnesota. They provide a descriptive and visual record of Native American life as he saw it, particularly among the Dakota. Mayer includes sketches of lacrosse, child rearing practices, smoking the peace pipe, buffalo dancers, teepees and summer lodges, and portraits of prominent leaders.

tribal lands were of little value to them. They were bereft of game and continuing to hold them would not improve a situation where "you and your children sometimes starve in summer and freeze in winter."[60]

Before outlining treaty terms, Lea assured the Sisseton and Wahpeton leaders that "I will not ask of you anything which your Great Father and I do not look upon as for your benefit." Perhaps to forestall any Indian hopes of bargaining with the commissioners, Lea made it clear that he and Ramsey were acting under instructions from their government.

On May 16, 1851, Secretary of the Interior Alexander H.H. Stuart had instructed Lea and Ramsey to acquire Dakota lands west of the Mississippi between the boundaries established by the Prairie du Chien treaties of 1825 and 1830. Furthermore, Stuart wrote that the government would not pay more than ten cents an acre and that he believed the land could be obtained for as little as four to five cents per acre. Within those guidelines Stuart gave the commissioners some discretion. But he was very firm relative to reservations and the payment of debts to traders. Neither were to be allowed, he dictated, because they were "expressly prohibited by a resolution of the Senate, passed on the 3d of March, 1843, which that body has subsequently refused to rescind."[62]

Despite Stuart's clear instructions about reservations, Lea and Ramsey decided to challenge both him and the Senate. In his opening talk to the Sisseton and Wahpeton leaders, Lea mentioned the government's willingness to pay a "fair price" for the lands and the creation of a reservation along the upper Minnesota River. He stated that the treaty would result in the Sisseton and Wahpeton getting an annual money income, blacksmith shops, farms, schools and medical facilities. Lea also proposed that the western boundary of their cession would be a line drawn from the mouth of the Buffalo River southward along the west bank of the Red and Bois des Sioux rivers to Lake Traverse. It would then follow the western shore of Lake Traverse to its south end and from that point run directly southwesterly to the point where the Big Sioux entered Lake Kampeska. From there to the northwest corner of Iowa the boundary would follow the Big Sioux's western bank.[63]

In explaining how such an agreement would benefit the Indians, Lea commented: "There are many other tribes of red men, who, like yourselves, once owned a large country—it was of no use to them, and they were poor; so they sold out to the Great Father, receiving therefore, goods, provisions, and money, with many other substantial benefits. Those tribes are now happier and more comfortable, and every year growing richer and richer. We hear of no starving among them. They always have plenty to eat, and enough to clothe them. Your Great Father wants to put an end, in like manner, to the suffering and poverty which has existed among you."[64]

In concluding their first session, Lea and Ramsey invited the chiefs to discuss their proposal among themselves "and meet us here again tomorrow, ready to go on with business."[65]

The next morning Lea and Ramsey announced the resumption of the conference by firing guns and hoisting flags. Once the meeting got underway at noon they were disappointed to learn that the only Indian reactions were complaints about inadequate representation. Wee-tchan-h' pee-ee-tay-toan (the "Star Face"), also identified by the whites as "The Orphan," chief of the Lake Traverse Sisseton band, spoke at length about how he wanted to wait for the arrival of some of his young men. Lea and Ramsey curtly responded that it would be a waste of time to wait for more Indians. Making the weather-related delay sound like the fault of the Dakotas, they stated that they had wanted to start negotiating on July 1, but the Indians had not arrived. They further asserted that the government required only the representation of chiefs and headmen, that Lea had to get back to Washington and that they did not have adequate food supplies for prolonged negotiations involving yet more people.[66]

Eesh-ta-hum-ba ("Sleepy Eyes"), chief of the Swan Lake Sisseton band, bluntly rejected the commissioners' explanation. He admonished them that "your coming and asking me for my country makes me sad; and your saying I am not able to do anything with my country, makes me more sad. Those who are coming behind are my near relatives and I expected certainly to see them here. That is all I have to say. I am going to leave, and that is the reason I spoke." Some other Sissetons, goaded by "loud cries from their young men on the outskirts" walked out with Sleepy Eyes.[67]

Lea and Ramsey reacted to the crisis swiftly and decisively. They ordered the striking of the council flag, the readying of their boats for departure and an immediate halt to the issuance of Indian rations. Lea, essentially acknowledging that they were bluffing, advised the chiefs that if they wanted to continue negotiating in earnest, they had to so inform the commissioners by that evening.[68]

The gambit worked. A few hours later a delegation of chiefs informed Lea and Ramsey that they wanted to continue talking and apologized for Sleepy Eyes' action. The commissioners promptly rescinded their orders to end the negotiations and, since the following day was a Sunday, to resume them on Monday, July 21.

In the Monday session, Lea and Ramsey met a very subdued group. Sleepy Eyes set the tone by apologizing for his previous conduct. Then Oo-pee-ya-hen-day-a ("Extending his Train"), known to the whites as "Curly Head," asked that the stipulations mentioned by Lea be put in writing so he and the other leaders could consider them. Lea did so. But, he then coerced Curly Head into proclaiming that the tribesmen intended to sell their lands, but were concerned only with the terms. Sensing his advantage, Lea bluntly told the chiefs and headmen that "if we do anything in regard to making a treaty here, it must be done quickly. You are not women and children, but men and chiefs, and ought to be able to act without delay, like men. We shall expect to hear your views decisively at our next meeting."[69]

Understanding treaty language was very difficult for the mostly illiterate chiefs and headmen. Consequently, they sought the advice of traders including Henry H. Sibley and Martin McLeod and missionary Stephen Return Riggs who was also acting as one of the conference interpreters. Le Duc reported that Sibley, McLeod and Riggs "and others are sent for at all hours of the day or night, to explain to the different bands the provisions of the treaty. . . ."[70] As the treaty's terms were explained to them, the chiefs and headmen realized they were being presented with an ultimatum. Collectively, they concluded it was better to sign and get something for their land rather than refuse and run the risk of simply having it taken from them.

Consequently, when the council resumed at 7:00 a.m. on Tuesday, July 22, the Wahpeton chief Een-yang-ma-nee ("He Whose Walk is Like Running," which whites usually abridged to "Running Walker,") also known as "The Gun" acted as spokesman for the group. He gave Lea a paper containing the terms under which the Indians would sell. Evidently, it was not substantially different than what Lea and Ramsey had offered, because after the brief meeting adjourned Lea and Ramsey began preparing for the signing ceremony the next day.[71]

The chiefs and headmen reportedly spent an anxious night discussing what they should do if Lea and Ramsey rejected their proposed changes. All concerned expected to perform the signing ceremony early on July 23. But threatening skies delayed the start until early afternoon.

Lea and Ramsey prepared for the signing ceremony by having gifts for the chiefs and headmen piled in a cor-

The Signing of the Treaty of Traverse des Sioux
by Francis Davis Millet (1846–1912), Oil ca. 1905
Painting in the Governor's Reception Room, State Capitol, from the collection of the Minnesota Historical Society

Francis Davis Millet, artist, was born in Mattapoisett, Mass, November 3, 1846; died in the sinking of the steamship *Titanic*, in the North Atlantic Ocean, April 15, 1912. He graduated from Harvard University, 1869; studied at the Royal Academy of Fine Arts, Antwerp, 1871–72.

ner of the council house. Le Duc reported them to be "goods and presents of various kinds—here a huge pile of various colored blankets, there red and blue cloths, looking glasses and ribbons, powder and lead, and hundreds of other items of utility or fancy." Mayer said the presents consisted of "blankets, cloth, powder, lead, tobacco, vermillion [sic], beads, looking glasses, knives, trinkets, etc."[72]

Once the final session was underway, Thomas Foster, the commission's secretary, read an English language copy of the treaty. Stephen Return Riggs, fluent in Dakota and the compiler of a Dakota-English dictionary, then read the text in Dakota.[73]

After the readings the colorfully painted chiefs and headmen led by Running Walker lined up to mark their acceptance on two copies of the treaty. Lea and Ramsey hoped that the signing would be routine. But as the Indian leaders queued up to accept the treaty, several of them paused long enough to express some misgivings. The Orphan, leery of federal government bureaucracy, said that "after it is signed, I desire it to remain unchanged and not go to Washington to be altered."[74] Curly Head, alert to how the infusion of cash would affect the Indians, stated: "Fathers—you think it is a great deal you are giving for this country. I don't think so; for both our lands and all we will get for them, will at last belong to the white man. The money comes to us, but will all go to the white men who trade with us...."[72]

Le Duc, who served as one of the treaty's witnesses, reported that several of the chiefs signed "their own names; having been taught to read and write in their own language by the Missionaries."[76] All the rest merely marked an X. It is impossible to identify those who were able to sign their own names, because the names of all signers had a subjoined X. Likewise, the degree of literacy of those who penned their names is not known. There is no evidence that it was sufficient to enable them to read the text of the treaty.

After marking the treaty copies the Indians were directed by Riggs toward an upright barrel where Joseph R. Brown had another document for them to accept. Brown not only did not explain the paper, but also rejected a suggestion by Dakota Indian agent Nathaniel McLean that it be read to the Indian leaders. Despite this alert that something was amiss, thirty-three of those who had signed the treaty copies affixed their marks to Brown's paper. Some of the signers may have assumed that the document was a third copy of the treaty. But, within hours they learned that it was a contract that obligated the Sisseton and Wahpeton bands to reimburse Sibley and his associates for outstanding individual debts of individual Indians.[77]

When the signing ceremony was completed, Lea and Ramsey presented the stockpiled gifts to the chiefs and headmen. This ritual was a continuation of the long-standing white practice that dated to colonial America of distributing gifts at treaty signings.[78]

Lea and Ramsey and their party, eager to move downstream to meet with the Mdewakanton and Wahpekute at Mendota, left by a Durham boat the day after the signing. The Dakota, whom the commissioners had given all remaining cattle, corn, flour and other foodstuffs gradually returned to their villages to await the Great Father's response to the treaty.[79]

When the Treaty of Traverse des Sioux was presented to the United States Senate for its consideration, it was accompanied by two other treaties made with Minnesota Indians in 1851. On July 29 Lea and Ramsey began meeting with Mdewakanton and Wahpekute chiefs and headmen at Mendota. The commissioners and the tribal leaders signed the Treaty of Mendota on August 5. Its monetary provisions generally mirrored those of the Treaty of Traverse des Sioux with stipulations for annual payments and agricultural and educational funds. The reservation designated for the Mdewakanton and Wahpekute was to be the same width as the Sisseton-Wahpeton reservation and extended on both sides of the Minnesota River from the Yellow Medicine River and Hawk Creek southeastward to the Little Rock River. Outside of the document, the Indians were induced to sign a traders' paper.[80]

After completing the Mendota treaty, Ramsey and an accompanying party, in accordance with Secretary of the Interior Stuart's instructions, journeyed to Pembina to negotiate a land cession with the Pembina and Red Lake bands of Ojibwe. The village of Pembina, on the west side of the Red River only about a mile south of the Canada-United States boundary, was the only place of note in the American portion of the Red River valley. Peopled mainly by Métis, Pembina had developed a trade with Norman

Kittson, one of Sibley's main agents. The Pembinian desire to acquire private land claims was the main reason for the contemplated Ojibwe cession. In 1851 there was no popular demand in St. Paul and environs to open the Red River valley as an agricultural frontier.[81]

After five days of preliminary feasting and talking, Ramsey and fifteen chiefs and headmen of the Pembina and Red Lake Ojibwe, signed a cession treaty on September 20. The bands ceded five million acres on both sides of the Red River for two cents an acre. The international boundary was the cession's northern limit. On the east side of the river the ceded lands consisted of an approximately thirty-mile wide strip south to the Buffalo River. A comparably-sized swath on the west side ran south to the Goose River.[82]

Part 5

Provisions of the Treaty of Traverse des Sioux and the Traders' Paper

The essence of the Treaty of Traverse des Sioux was that the Sisseton and Wahpeton bands of Dakota would cede their lands to the United States for a reservation along the upper Minnesota River and various payments.

There is no record that Lea and Ramsey ever explained just what lands were involved. They were content in their knowledge that the southern boundary of the Dakota had been established by the 1830 Treaty of Prairie du Chien, the eastern boundary by the half-breed tract provision in the same treaty, the Pike Treaty and the Mdewakanton cession of 1837, and the northern boundary by the Dakota-Ojibwe boundary stipulated in the 1825 Treaty of Prairie du Chien. Rather than reiterate these particulars, the Treaty of Traverse des Sioux merely stipulated that the Sisseton and Wahpeton ceded "all of their lands in the State of Iowa; and, also all their lands in the Territory of Minnesota...." But since no western boundary for Dakota claims had ever been set prior to

Traverse des Sioux, the treaty provided that it would mostly be a water line formed by the Red, Bois des Sioux and Big Sioux rivers and Lake Traverse from the mouth of the Buffalo River to the northwest corner of Iowa. From the southern end of Lake Traverse, the source of the Bois des Sioux River, the boundary was to be a direct line overland southwesterly to the point where the Big Sioux River entered the north side of Lake Kampeska near the western edge of present-day Watertown, South Dakota. This western boundary line was acceptable to the Indian signers because they acknowledged that the lands west of it belonged to the Nakota (i.e. the Middle Sioux composed of the Yankton and Yanktonai bands). But the government did not consult with the Nakota, but merely established their eastern boundary by the Treaty of Traverse des Sioux.

To determine how much land was ceded by the Dakota in 1851 it is necessary to combine the Traverse des Sioux and Mendota cessions, because there was no boundary separating the lands of the upper Sioux and the lower Sioux. There was no reason for one. The four Dakota bands, which had the same language, culture and mores freely intermixed and intermarried. Obviously the upper Sioux would have been much more prevalent in the western portion of the Dakota lands and the lower Sioux in the eastern part. The lack of a demarcation between the upper and lower Sioux lands was shown by the Treaty of Mendota, which the Mdewakanton and Wahpekute chiefs and headmen signed on August 5, 1851. They agreed to "cede and relinquish all their lands and

Territory Ceded by the 1851 Dakota Treaties

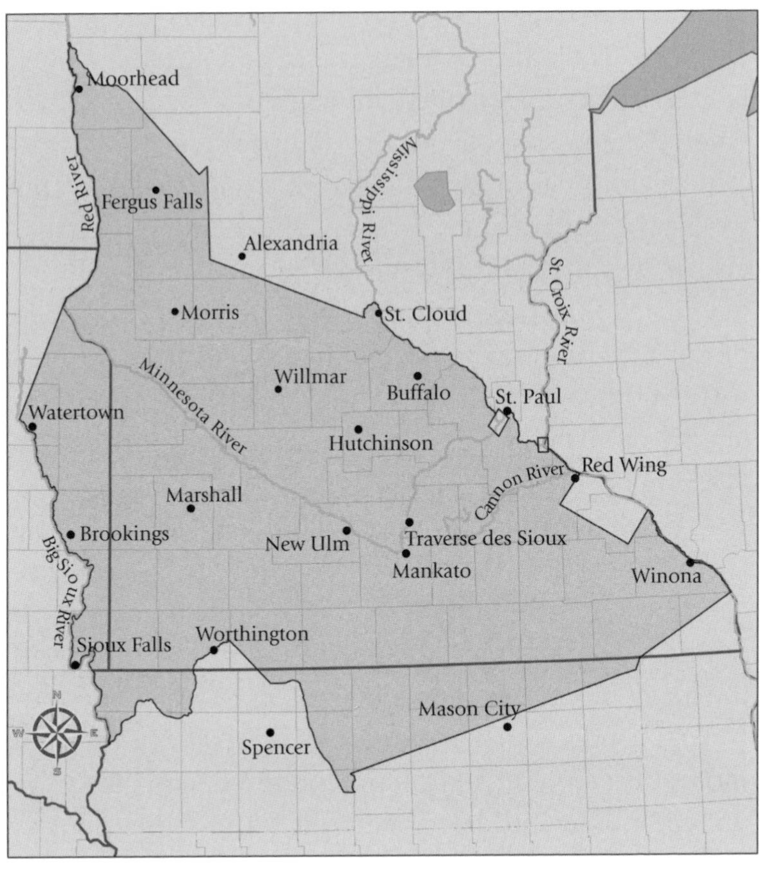

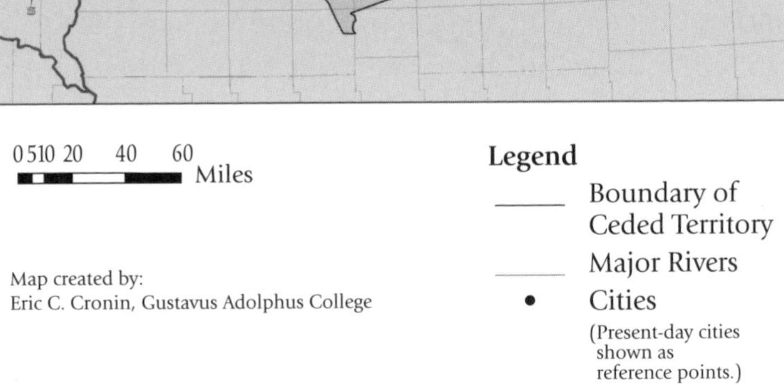

Map created by:
Eric C. Cronin, Gustavus Adolphus College

Dakota Reservations on the Upper Minnesota River

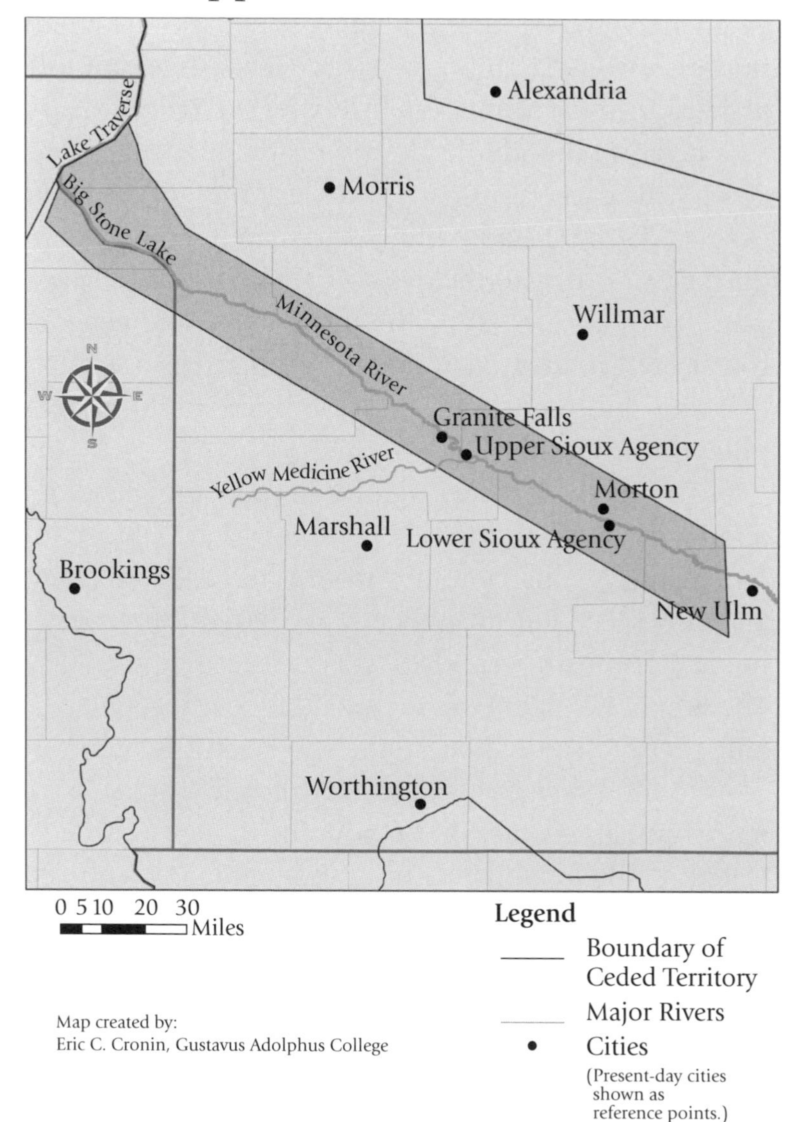

all their right, title and claim to any lands whatever, in the Territory of Minnesota, or in the State of Iowa."[83]

Within the ceded area, the Treaty of Traverse des Sioux stipulated that the Sissetons and Wahpetons would be granted a reservation extending southeastward from the cession's western boundary to Hawk Creek on the north side of the Minnesota River and the Yellow Medicine River on the south side and nearly opposite Hawk Creek. This tract was to extend "on each side" of the Minnesota River "a distance of not less than ten miles from the general course of the river...." which was southeastward. In practical terms, this meant that the general course of the Minnesota would be calculated by a straight line and the reservation's outside lines would be ten miles on either side of it.

The United States agreed to pay the Sisseton and Wahpeton bands $1,665,000 for their cession. In 2010 dollars this amount would be an estimated $43,806,150.[84] But this was not an outright lump payment. Portions it were dedicated to specific purposes. The sum of $275,000 was to be paid to the chiefs "to enable them to settle their affairs," to cover the removal costs to the reservation and to provide one year's subsistence for their people. Thirty thousand dollars were dedicated to "the establishment of manual-labor schools; the erection of mills and blacksmith shops, opening farms, fencing and breaking land, and for such other beneficial objects as may be deemed most conducive to the prosperity and happiness of said Indians...." In other words, this was money that the Indians would not see.

The government, through its Indian service, would use the funds for such things as establishing the named facilities and employing white men to act as reservation farmers and skilled laborers.

After deducting the cost of the first two items, there was a balance of $1,360,000. This amount was "to remain in trust with the United States, and five per cent interest ($68,000) thereon" was to be paid to the Indians annually for fifty years. The government retained control of over a fourth of the annual payments by specifying $12,000 was to be devoted to "agricultural improvements and civilization" and $6,000 for the establishment and maintenance of reservation schools. Whether the Indians realized it or not, the creation of these two funds indicated the government intended to convert them to the white lifestyle.

The remaining $50,000 from the interest income was to be paid as annuities in the form of goods and cash. One-fifth was to be spent on goods and four-fifths was to be cash distributed to the heads of families.

The obligation the chiefs and headmen undertook by signing the traders' paper was not part of the treaty, but in the minds of the Indians, especially, it was always associated with the treaty. Whether the signing of the paper was a legitimate way of resolving Indian indebtedness to the traders or an underhanded dirty trick is open to interpretation.

Those involved in the treaty including the traders, the commissioners and the Indians knew that various Sisseton and Wahpeton individuals owed money to Sibley or traders associated with him. At least a year before the treaty some of Sibley's traders tried to persuade some chiefs that they should use treaty income to repay the traders. Lea, Ramsey and Sibley, who were at least knowledgeable about recent Indian history, knew that allowances for debt repayment had once been a regular feature in treaties, such as the Mdewakanton cession of 1837. But probably because of public opposition to such stipulations, which were regarded as special interest benefits, the Senate in 1843 banned debt repayment provisions in treaties. This action was reinforced by a comparable provision in an act concerning organization of the Indian Department approved by Congress on March 3, 1847.

The congressional enactment seemingly left the traders with no means of collecting their debts. Traditional legal methods such as suing debtors obviously were not feasible in this situation.

The seeming Ewing threat was another cause of concern for Sibley and those associated with him. When Sibley and some of his main associates including Hercules Dousman of Prairie du Chien, Wisconsin, Joseph R. Brown, Alexander Faribault and Martin McLeod dallied at Traverse des Sioux awaiting the commencement of negotiations, they were perturbed by the presence of Richard Chute. The former Ewing brothers agent in Iowa, Chute had entered Minnesota in 1850 when he supervised part of the Winnebago removal. He attracted much attention at Traverse des Sioux because he was somewhat of an outcast among the small white contingent and also because he was accompanied by his attractive wife, Mary A., the encampment's only white woman. Chute, obviously cowered by the Sibley group and the very apparent friendship between Sibley and the commissioners, merely observed the treaty preliminaries and negotiations. Nonetheless, as long as he was present, Sibley and his group were uncertain about his intentions.[86]

The combination of the congressional ban and the feared Ewing incursion caused the Sibley group to become innovative by resorting to the traders' paper. Lea and Ramsey were aware that the paper would be proposed and created the opportunity to advance it by stipulating funding in the treaty that would enable the chiefs "to settle their affairs and comply with their present just engagement. . . ." Ramsey was later accused by Madison Sweetser, a Ewing agent, of having colluded with the traders. But he was cleared by a Senate investigating committee after it determined he had no role in preparing the paper and was unaware of its particulars. Significantly, Ramsey defended the use of the traders' paper, because of the key role played by the traders in convincing the Indians to negotiate the treaty.

Sisseton and Wahpeton objections to the traders' paper were more concerned with its administration rather than its principle. Some of the chiefs, influenced by their societal norms whereby tribesmen regularly provided for their kinsmen, did not protest the idea of the paper. But they complained it had not been explained to them in advance and that they were tricked into signing it. Both contentions have merit. The paper, by which the chiefs and headmen agreed to reimburse the traders to the extent of $431,735.78 was not shown to the Indians before the signing ceremony. Furthermore, neither Riggs nor Brown identified it before asking the Indians to accept it. It is quite understandable that some of them thought like missionary Thomas Williamson, an eyewitness to the event, that it was a third copy of the treaty.[87]

Shortly after the paper was signed the traders learned that its total amount far exceeded the treaty's allowance. That same afternoon a committee of three traders—Brown, McLeod and Louis Robert—reduced the payment to $210,000. That evening and night various traders including Sibley, who recalled working into the candlelight hours, showed the changes to the chiefs. The next day a list of the Indian payments due each trader was attached to the paper.

Some Sissetons and Wahpetons were so upset with the traders' paper affair that they followed the commissioners to Mendota to protest. But they were summarily rejected. This experience further embittered them about the entire treaty-making process.

PART 6
Implementing the Treaty of Traverse des Sioux

Both the whites and Dakotas in Minnesota anxiously awaited federal government reaction to the Traverse des Sioux and Mendota treaties. But over the months they came to realize that the president and the Senate did not see any urgency in the matter. Congress was adjourned from March 3 to December 1, 1851. Then after the Thirty-second Congress convened on December 1, President Millard Fillmore waited until February 13, 1852, before sending the Dakota treaties and the Pembina treaty to the Senate.[88]

Three days later the Senate referred the treaties to its Committee on Indian Affairs chaired by Senator David R. Atchison of Missouri. Atchison reported back to the Senate on April 19 with the recommendations that the Treaty of Traverse des Sioux be approved as negotiated, that the Treaty of Mendota be amended to delete the eighth article relating to a half-breed payment and that the Pembina treaty be rejected.

After first discussing the Treaty of Traverse des Sioux on May 3, the Senate did not resume consideration of it until June 9. By that time Minnesota's pro-Dakota treaties sentiment was evident to the Senate. Various senators had presented six petitions from Minnesotans asking that the Dakota treaties be approved. Senators could not help but notice the public's lack of enthusiasm for the Ojibwe treaty, which made it easy for them to not even consider it as a body.

During the Senate discussion of June 9–11, it became obvious that there was strong opposition to the Treaty of Traverse des Sioux. Minnesota historian William Watts Folwell suggested that the rejection movement came from Southerners, who wanted to delay the addition of another free state to the union. But an analysis of Senate votes shows the issue was considerably more complicated. It is true that most of the treaty's supporters were Northerners and most of its opponents were Southerners, but sectional loyalties did not extend to the point of voting as a bloc. Apparently, some of the opposition came from senators who were offended by the traders' paper deal or who were interested in reforming the Indian treaty system.[89]

On June 9 Atchison moved to delete article 3, which provided for the upper Minnesota valley reservation, from the Treaty of Traverse des Sioux. This action was hardly surprising because Lea and Ramsey in establishing the reservation had flaunted both the Senate's ban and Stuart's instructions. Nonetheless, the reservation as negotiated by Lea and Ramsey had considerable support. The Senate approved the deletion of the reservation article by a close vote of 25 to 19.[90]

Obviously, the deletion of article 3 left a void that had to be filled. Atchison responded promptly. On June 11 he proposed a supplemental article stipulating that the government would purchase from the Sissetons and Wahpetons the reservation designated in article 3 for ten cents an acre. Furthermore, the article specified that the president "with the assent of the said band of Indians, parties to this treaty" could establish a reservation for them outside of the lands they had ceded. But rather than make this hard and firm, the article offered another option by providing "that the President may, by the consent of these Indians, vary the conditions aforesaid if deemed expedient."[91] The supplemental article was the most popular feature of the Senate's consideration of the treaty. It was overwhelmingly approved by a 41 to 4 vote.[92]

On June 22 Atchison moved that the Senate "advise and consent to the ratification of the articles" of the Treaty of Traverse des Sioux by deleting article 3 and adding the supplemental article. The Senate barely approved by a vote of 25 to 12. Since the constitution stipulated that treaties had to be approved by a two-thirds vote of all members present, one less aye or one more nay would have resulted in the treaty's rejection. Of course, a rejection would not have precluded a reconsideration. As expected the vote indicated sectional differences. Of the twelve negative votes cast, six were by senators from states that later joined the Confederacy, four were by senators from slave states that did not join the Confederacy and two were by senators from free states. But the vote clearly shows that Southerners were not united. Six senators from states that later joined the Confederacy voted for the treaty as did one senator from a slave state that did not join the Confederacy. If all senators had voted their seeming sectional interest, the treaty would never have been approved. The nay votes by Richard Brodhead of Pennsylvania and Hamilton Fish of New York indicate motives for opposing the treaty other than the desire to delay Minnesota statehood.[93]

The closeness of the Traverse des Sioux vote and the Senate's high absentee rate greatly concerned Dakota treaty advocates. Consequently, they drummed up support for the Treaty of Mendota. On June 23 when the Senate voted on the Mendota treaty, which had reservation provisions parallel to the Traverse des Sioux document, it was approved by a vote of 31 to 13.

As approved by the Senate the Treaty of Traverse des Sioux was somewhat tenuous. Before it could go into effect the government acting through Alexander Ramsey as Minnesota's ex-officio superintendent of Indian affairs and the Dakotas had to agree on a reservation site. Despite the supplemental article's clear preference for a reservation outside of Minnesota, Ramsey apparently never seriously considered it. By corresponding through Luke Lea he appealed to President Fillmore to permit the Dakotas to temporarily occupy the reservations originally assigned to them by the treaties of Traverse des Sioux and Mendota. Although the administration agreed to this, Ramsey also wanted to preclude any possible Senate opposition. So he sought and obtained from Senator Atchison an assurance that the Senate would allow a reservation to be established within the ceded lands. Ramsey then followed the most convenient path by deciding to fix the reservation's boundaries exactly as had been specified in the deleted third article.[94]

Ramsey also had to deal with the potentially troublesome supplemental article's stipulation that the Senate's changes to the Treaty of the Traverse des Sioux had to be approved by the affected Dakotas. He realized that, because of his participation in the treaty negotiations and the traders' paper transaction, the chiefs were likely to reject any overture from him. Ramsey solved his dilemma by enlisting the services of Henry Mower Rice, a veteran trader and Sibley's political rival. Rice had let it be known that for a $10,000 fee he would persuade the Dakotas to accept the Senate changes. Although he was well-known as persuasive deal maker, Rice had only limited experience with the Dakota. But, confident of his understanding of Indian character, he met with delegations of chiefs at Mendota and Traverse des Sioux in September, 1852. For unrecorded reasons, he convinced the chiefs it was to their benefit to accept the Senate changes and the assurance of the reservations specified in the original 1851 treaties. Ramsey, Sibley and other treaty supporters had worried about the supplemental article's requirement that the Dakotas had to assent to the changes. Rice finessed the issue by interpreting the stipulation to mean that the signatures of representative chiefs would suffice. Once he obtained them, Ramsey and other government officials accepted his action.[95]

Following Rice's effort, Ramsey, working partially through a hired agent, negotiated the traders' paper settlements with both lower and upper Dakota chiefs. These details extended into the late fall of 1852. As long as any matters involving the treaties of Traverse des Sioux and Mendota were unresolved, President Fillmore refrained from approving the treaties. Finally, on February 24, 1853, he proclaimed them to be in effect. Thus, the Treaty of Traverse des Sioux, which had been signed on July 23, 1851, was in limbo for over a year and a half.

Legally, the lands ceded by the treaties of Traverse des Sioux and Mendota were not added to the federal public domain until the president approved the treaties. But early white Minnesotans, like frontier people elsewhere in the nation, were an impatient sort. In the areas closest to St. Paul, settlers rushed onto the Dakota lands right after the Treaty of Mendota had been signed. While they were acting illegally, the federal government had neither the power nor the will to expel them. The easiest course for government officials was to assume that all would soon be alright because the treaties would be rapidly approved.[96]

The illegal quest for Dakota lands was extended to the Minnesota River valley in 1851 when townsite speculators founded Shakopee and Chaska. The next year various developers and companies, operating out of St. Paul, started the towns of Henderson, Le Sueur, Traverse des Sioux and Mankato. In the case of Mankato, Sleepy Eyes objected to the intrusion of his domain, but permitted it after townsite company agents gave him some supplies.[97]

As these towns were being started, many settlers made land claims in the Minnesota Triangle—the area south of St. Paul between the Mississippi and Minnesota rivers. By the end of 1852, an estimated 5,000 whites had moved into the region.[98]

As word of the approval of the Traverse des Sioux and Mendota treaties spread in the late winter and spring of 1853, increasing numbers of white settlers occupied parts of the recently ceded lands. But they found that the indigenous Dakotas were reluctant to move out. This problem of a continuing Dakota presence was particularly acute in areas occupied by the Mdewankanton and Wahpekute. As traditional forest dwellers, they naturally resisted moving onto the unfamiliar prairies, where a subagency was being prepared for them on the south side of the Minnesota River about seven miles southeast of the tributary Redwood River. Some of the Sissetons, such as those residing at Traverse des Sioux and Swan Lake, also had to relocate. But, unlike the lower Dakotas they had extensive prairie experience. Many of the upper Dakota, including the important Lac qui Parle and Lake Traverse bands, did not have to move, because they were already living within the designated reservation boundaries.[99]

The task of persuading the Dakotas to accept reservation life fell to Willis A. Gorman, who had succeeded Ramsey as territorial governor and ex-officio superintendent of Indian affairs. Gorman of Indiana was appointed by the incoming Democratic President Franklin

Pierce, who in keeping with the spoils system precedent, replaced the Whig Indian service incumbents. If nothing else, Gorman was persistent. By the late fall of 1853 he had coaxed the majority of the lower Dakotas to move to their reservation. Many of them stayed only long enough to receive annuities before returning to their old homes.

The failure of the Dakotas to accept the reservations as permanent, year-round homes is not too surprising. As a traditional semi-nomadic hunting society they were accustomed to ranging over wide areas. Furthermore, the government never really intended that they were to be confined within reservation boundaries. The troops at Fort Ridgely, which was established in 1853 about twelve miles southeast of the lower reservation agency , did not try to keep the Indians on the reservations. Indeed, the army and the Dakotas did not know the exact reservation boundaries, which were not finally surveyed and marked until 1859.

Despite the fluid reservation boundaries, the 1853 removal was symbolically important. Legally, it marked the beginning of a new era, in which the Dakotas held no rights to their ancestral lands outside of the reservations. Over the years as whites rushed onto the ceded lands the Dakotas had to acknowledge that the treaties of Traverse des Sioux and Mendota had limited them to only a small portion of their former space.

Part 7

Legacy of the Treaty of Traverse des Sioux

Understandably, white Minnesota settlers and traditionally-minded Dakotas held contrasting viewpoints on the Treaty of Traverse des Sioux. Generally, whites saw the treaty as a natural step in their inevitable, godly-ordained conquest of the wilderness. Traditional Dakotas, however, regarded it as the epochal event that ended their "good old days" and ushered in a dark age of Indian decline.

The most immediate effect of the Dakota treaties was an unprecedented Minnesota land rush with the greatest gains occurring in 1855 and 1856. An official 1855 census showed a population of 53,600 and an 1857 pre-statehood census reported 150,037 non-Indian inhabitants. The dramatic increase was fueled by the lure of widely acclaimed cheap, fertile land and a salubrious climate. Other contributing factors were the completion of a railroad from the east coast to Rock Island, Illinois, on the Mississippi and a booming national economy heavily dependent on land speculation.[100]

The land rush stimulated town and county formation. All of today's major cities in the Minnesota Triangle were founded between the negotiation of the Traverse des Sioux treaty and Minnesota's admission to the union on May 11, 1858. Minnesota Territory originally had only nine counties, but that number increased to 23 in 1854 and 63 three years later. When Minnesota became a state nearly all of its white population was located south of a line from Taylors Falls on the St. Croix to Little Falls on the Mississippi and east of a Little Falls-St. Cloud-Hutchinson-New Ulm-Fairmont line.

While white Minnesotans were enjoying their progress in settling the land, many of the reservation Dakotas were becoming increasingly disenchanted with their new way of life. From the start the government through missionaries encouraged the Dakotas to convert to a white lifestyle, which entailed abandoning Indian traditions and becoming like white Christian farmers whose men cut their hair short, dressed in work clothes and sometimes Sunday suits and spoke English. This assimilation program was accelerated after the former fur trader Joseph R. Brown was appointed Dakota agent in 1857. Brown was so determined to rapidly change the Dakota that he engineered their sale to the federal government of the northern half of both the upper and lower Dakota reservations in 1858. Proceeds from the sales were used to promote the construction of brick houses and to stimulate farming by Dakotas.[101]

The effect of Brown's program was to cause a serious rift in Dakota society. Some Dakotas, believing their best course was to become absorbed in white society, converted to Christianity and took up farming. But, others clung to their traditional gods, their old customs and a glorification of the pre-white days. The schism between the progressives (or "civilized" Indians as the whites called them) and the traditionalists (called "uncivilized" by the whites) not only ruined tribal unity, but inflamed hatred of whites among the traditionalists.

As Dakota society changed, the 1851 treaties, in retrospect, looked like a very bad deal to the white haters. Many of them believed they had been cheated out of their land and were destined to a ruinous future.

Lingering discontent over the treaties and Brown's assimilation program have been identified as significant long range causes of the Dakota War of 1862. But this animosity toward the government and white settlers probably would have smoldered, but never ignited, without the triggering events of 1861–62. The government's tardy issuance of annuities and its failure to provide relief to hundreds of desperately hungry Dakotas caused a traditionalist faction to launch attacks on nearby white settlers.[102]

The Dakota War was a disaster for both whites and the Dakotas. Approximately 450–500 whites were killed and most of the farming frontier ranging from St. Cloud to Fairmont was abandoned. Although white authorities did try, convict and execute some Dakota men for war crimes, all of the Dakotas suffered from the war. Historians have generally concluded that the Dakota war faction was dominated by Mdewakanton chiefs and warriors. The overwhelming majority of Sissetons and Wahpetons were either non-participants or pro-whites.

But, no society is capable of having a rational discussion of a war's causes in its immediate aftermath.

Consequently, white Minnesotans generally reacted harshly against all Dakotas. Goaded by public opinion and strident newspaper commentaries, Minnesota's congressional delegation proposed that all Dakotas be exiled from the state. Congress complied with two acts. On February 16, 1863, the legislators approved a law establishing a Sioux Claims Commission, which was authorized to reimburse victims for property losses caused by warring Sioux. Among other things the act specified that all treaties made between the United States and the lower and upper Dakota bands "are hereby declared to be abrogated and annulled, so far as said treaties or any of them purport to impose any future obligation on the United States, and all lands and rights of occupancy within the State of Minnesota, and all annuities and claims heretofore accorded to said Indians, or any of them, to be forfeited to the United States." Congress followed this with an act of March 3, 1863, which stipulated that the Dakota people were to be re-located to a new reservation outside the limits of any state. The law also provided that the lands in the two reservations along the upper Minnesota River be sold at public auction. The proceeds from the sales were to be used to support the Dakotas in their new home.[103]

Obviously only those Dakotas who had been captured or who had voluntarily surrendered could be removed. Over the winter of 1862–63 about 1,500 of them were confined in an encampment near Fort Snelling. In

May, 1863, they were removed by steamboat to the Crow Creek Reservation along the Missouri River in Dakota Territory. Most of those exiles were Mdewakantons, but Sissetons and Wahpetons comprised about one-fourth of the group.[104]

It is ironic that the Treaty of Traverse des Sioux is usually considered a background cause of the Dakota War. As a general rule, the Sissetons and Wahpetons who were affected by the treaty did not participate in the war. Nonetheless, realizing the anti-Indian frenzy that the Dakota War had unleashed, most of them fled westward out of Minnesota. Several hundred along with some Mdewakantons and Wahpekutes moved into Canada where they were later placed on reserves in Manitoba and Saskatchewan by the Dominion government.[105]

But, the largest Sisseton and Wahpeton groups moved onto the Dakota plains between Big Stone Lake and Devils Lake. In 1867, the federal government, by a treaty negotiated in Washington, D.C., assigned them to two new reservations. The first reservation for some 1,200 to 1,500 people was located in the northeastern part of later South Dakota. The second reservation for an estimated 1,000 to 1,200 Sissetons and Wahpetons was in land adjoining Devils Lake in later North Dakota. The treaty acknowledged that the two groups of Sissetons and Wahpetons had not only remained peaceful during the Dakota War, but had oftentimes assisted white settlers.[106]

In the nearly century and half since the Dakota War, contrasting white and Dakota views of the Treaty of Traverse des Sioux have persisted. Whites have generally seen the treaty as the event that launched Minnesota's development into a prosperous state. The frontier experience, which included the loss of land by the native people, has been an object of continuing fascination to the first white settlers and their successors. In 1903 when the celebrated architect Cass Gilbert was supervising the final touches of Minnesota's new state capitol, he wanted to furnish the building with paintings depicting famous episodes in Minnesota's history. At the suggestion of the Minnesota Historical Society, he decided to include a striking oil painting of the Treaty of Traverse des Sioux. Frank B. Mayer, who had done a painting of the treaty, had died in 1899. Consequently, Gilbert commissioned the well-known American artist and journalist Francis D. Millet to do a painting based on Mayer's depiction. Although Millet had painted a number of murals in public buildings throughout the country, his rendering of the Treaty of Traverse des Sioux, which involved over sixty figures, was said to be his most ambitious work. Over the years the Millet painting has been mainly responsible for the image Minnesotans have of the treaty.[107]

But the Treaty of Traverse des Sioux has also left a vivid impression on the Dakota memory of it. In recent times, Robert Clouse, head of the Minnesota Historical Society's Archaeology Department asked Paul Little, the tribal historian of the Devils Lake Sioux Tribe: "What was the effect of the Treaty of Traverse des Sioux on the Dakota and what is the feeling about that document today." Little responded: "The Treaty of Traverse des Sioux of 1851 was the one treaty that broke up the

Dakota people. It symbolized the loss of our land.... Even today, over 140 years later, this document continues to carry bitter feelings among the Dakota."[108]

Regardless of one's perspective, there is a general recognition that the Treaty of Traverse des Sioux was one of the most significant events in Minnesota's history. But, as with any other single happening, there are hazards in contemplating it without proper consideration of its broader context. Studied alone, the treaty seems to be very unique. But, for better or for worse, there is much truth in the comment by interpreter William L. Quinn that the treaties of Traverse des Sioux and Mendota "were as fair as any Indian treaties."[109] Quinn was, of course, looking at the Treaty of Traverse des Sioux from a frontier perspective. Consequently, he compared it to other cession treaties of its age with respect to the price the government paid for the land and the blunt methods used by Lea and Ramsey. The government justified the approximate price of a dime an acre on the grounds that the land was of no use to the Dakotas. As years passed treaty critics tended to think in terms of the actual market value of the land in a white society. At the time the Treaty of Traverse des Sioux was negotiated, federal public land auctions were required to open the bidding at $1.25 an acre.

Until 1871 when it discontinued the Indian treaty system, the United States Senate approved some 370 Indian treaties. The Senate rejected approximately another 45 that had been negotiated and signed in the field.

Therefore, Indian treaties were commonplace in the American experience.[110]

Although the Treaty of Traverse des Sioux bears striking similarities to other cession treaties, it has a special place in Minnesota's history. As the first major Dakota land cession west of the Mississippi, it opened Minnesota's prime agricultural lands to settlement. Thus, it has come to be regarded as an important symbol of white progress. Conversely, to the Dakotas it was the watershed event that ended their claims to a vast area. Although the Treaty of Traverse des Sioux has to be considered with the Treaty of Mendota, as the first one to be negotiated in 1851 it will always hold a special place. Its rural site is another factor that has magnified the Treaty of Traverse des Sioux. With its present-day metropolitan location, the Treaty of Mendota site is paled by such nearby historic sites as the restored and reconstructed Fort Snelling.

But the Traverse des Sioux site is removed from any other major reminder of Minnesota's past. The Nicollet County Historical Society certainly recognized the special place of the Treaty of Traverse des Sioux in the history of the Minnesota River valley and the psyche of its residents when it opened the Treaty Site History Center in 1994. Standing only a fourth of a mile from the spot where the Treaty of Traverse des Sioux was negotiated, the Center offers an excellent opportunity for all Minnesotans and others interested in regional history, Indians as well as whites, to learn about their collective past.

Original Traverse des Sioux Treaty Site and Treaty Rock.

The rock, still in this position today, located on Old Minnesota Avenue $^4/_{10}$ of a mile north of the Dodd Road intersection, marks the site of the signing of the Treaty of Traverse des Sioux in 1851. Members of the St. Peter D.A.R. arranged for the rock to be brought to the site. With an attached plaque, the rock was dedicated in 1914. Postcard negative, marked 459, from the collection of the Nicollet County Historical Society.

PART 8

Appendix: Copy of the Treaty of Traverse des Sioux

Articles of a treaty made and concluded at Traverse des Sioux, upon the Minnesota River, in the Territory of Minnesota, on the twenty-third day of July, eighteen hundred and fifty-one, between the United States of America, by Luke Lea, Commissioner of Indian Affairs, and Alexander Ramsey governor and ex-officio superintendent of Indian affairs in said Territory, commissioners duly appointed for that purpose, and See-see-toan and Wah-pay-toan bands of Dakota or Sioux Indians.

ARTICLE 1. It is stipulated and solemnly agreed that the peace and friendship now so happily existing between the United States and the aforesaid bands of Indians, shall be perpetual.

ARTICLE 2. The said See-see-toan and Wah-pay-toan bands of Dakota or Sioux Indians, agree to cede, and do hereby cede, sell, and relinquish to the United States, all of their lands in the State of Iowa; and, also all their lands in the Territory of Minnesota, lying east of the following line, to wit: Beginning at the junction of the

Buffalo River with the Red River of the North; thence along the western bank of said Red River of the North, to the mouth of the Sioux Wood [Bois des Sioux] River; thence along the western bank of said Sioux Wood River to Lake Traverse; thence, along the western shore of said lake, to the southern extremity thereof; thence in a direct line, to the junction of Kampeska Lake with the Tchan-kas-an-data, or Sioux River; thence along the western bank of said river to its point of intersection with the northern line of the State of Iowa; including all the islands in said rivers and lake.

ARTICLE 3. [Stricken out.]

ARTICLE 4. In further and full consideration of said cession, the United States agree to pay to said Indians the sum of one million six hundred and sixty-five thousand dollars ($1.665,000,) at the several times, in the manner and for the purposes following, to wit:

1st. To the chiefs of the said bands, to enable them to settle their affairs and comply with their present just engagement; and in consideration of their removing themselves to the country set apart for them as above, which they agree to do within two years, or sooner, if required by the President, without further cost or expense to the United States, and in consideration of their subsisting themselves the first year after their removal, which they agree to do without further cost or expense on the part of the United States, the sum of two hundred seventy-five thousand dollars, ($275,000): *Provided,* That said sum shall be paid to the chiefs in such manner as they, hereafter, in open council shall request, and as soon after the removal of said Indians to the home set apart for them, as the necessary appropriation therefor *[sic]* shall be made by Congress.

2d. To be laid out under the direction of the President for the establishment of manual-labor schools; the erection of mills and blacksmith shops, opening farms, fencing and breaking land, and for such other beneficial objects as may be deemed most conducive to the prosperity and happiness of the Indians, thirty thousand dollars, ($30,000.)

The balance of said sum of one million six hundred and sixty-five thousand dollars, ($1,650,000) to wit: one million three hundred and sixty thousand dollars ($1,360,000) to remain in trust with the United States, and five per cent. Interest thereon to be paid, annually , to said Indians for the period of fifty years, commencing the first day of July, eighteen hundred and fifty-two (1852,) which shall be in full payment of said balance, principal and interest, the said payment to be applied under the direction of the President, as follows, to wit:

3d. For the general agricultural improvement and civilization fund, the sum of twelve thousand dollars, ($12,000.)

4th. For educational purposes, the sum of six thousand dollars, ($6,000.)

5th. For the purchase of goods and provisions, the sum of ten thousand dollars, ($10,000).

6th. For money annuity, the sum of forty thousand dollars, ($40,000).

ARTICLE 5. The laws of the United States prohibiting the introduction and sale of spirituous liquors in the Indian country shall be in full force and effect throughout the territory hereby ceded and lying in Minnesota until otherwise directed by Congress or the President of the United States.

ARTICLE 6. Rules and regulations to protect the rights of persons and property among the Indians, parties to this treaty, and adapted to their condition and wants, may be prescribed and enforced in such manner as the President or the Congress of the United States, from time to time shall direct.

In testimony whereof, the said Commissioners, Luke Lea and Alexander Ramsey, and the undersigned Chiefs and Headmen of the aforesaid See-see-toan and Wah-pay-toan bands of Dakota or Sioux Indians, have hereunto subscribed their names and affixed their seals, in duplicate, at Traverse des Sioux, Territory of Minnesota, this twenty-third day of July, one thousand eight hundred and fifty-one.

L. Lea, [SEAL,]

Alex. Ramsey, [SEAL,]

Een-yang-ma-nee, (Running Walker or "the Gun,")

Wee-tchan-h' pee-ee-tay-toan (the Star face or the "Orphan,")

Ee-tay-wa-keen-yan, ("Limping Devil" or "Thunder Face,")

Eesh-ta-hum-ba, ("Sleepy Eyes,")

Oo-pee-ya-hen-day-a, (Extending his train,)
Hoak-shee-dan-wash-tay, (Good Boy,)
Ee-tay-tcho-ka, (Face in the midst,)
Hay-ha-hen-day-ma-za, (Metal Horn,)
Am-pay-too-sha, (Red Day,)
Eesh-ta-humba-koash-ka, (Sleepy Eyes young,)
A na-wang-ma-nee, (Who goes galloping on,)
Ma-h' pee-wee-tchash-ta, (Cloud man,)
Tan-pa-hee-da, (Sounding Moccasin,)
Eenk-pa, (the upper end,)
Wee-yoa-kee-yay, (Standard,)
Wa-kan-ma-nee, (Walking Spirit,)
Ee-tay-sha, (the one that reddens his face,)
Ta-ka-ghay, (Elk maker,)
Wa-ma-ksoon-tay, ("Walnut," or Blunt headed arrow,)
Ma-za-sh'a, (Metal Sounding,)
Ya-shoa-pee, (The wind instrument,)
Noan-pa-keen-yan, (Twice Flying,)
Wash-tay-da, (Good, a little,)
Wa-keen-yan-ho-ta, (Grey Thunder,)
Wa-shee-tchoon-ma-za, (Iron Frenchman,)
Ta-pe-ta-tan-ka, (His Big Fire,)
Ma-h' pee-ya-h' na-shkan-shkan, (Moving Cloud,)
Wa-na-pay-a, (The pursuer,)

Ee-tcha-shkan-shkan-ma-nee, (Who walks shaking,)

Ta-wa-kan-he-day-ma-za, (His Metal Lightning,)

Ee-tay-doo-ta, (Red Face,)

Henok-marpi-yahdi-nape, (Reappearing Cloud,)

Tchan-hedaysh-ka-ho-toan-ma-nee,
(the moving sounding Harp,)

Ma-zaku-te-ma-ni, (Metal walks shooting,)

A-kee-tchee-ta, (Standing Soldier,)

Signed in presence of Thomas Foster, Secretary. Nathaniel McLean, Indian Agent. Alexander Faribault, Stephen R. Riggs, Interpreters. A.S.H. White; Thos. S. Williamson; W.C. Henderson; A. Jackson; James W. Boal; W.G. Le Duc; Alexis Bailly; H.L. Dousman; Hugh Tyler.

To the Indian names are subjoined marks.

SUPPLEMENTAL ARTICLE.

1st. The United States do hereby stipulate to pay the Sioux bands of Indians, parties to this treaty, at the rate of ten cents per acre, for the lands included in the reservation provided for in the third article of the treaty as originally agreed upon in the following words:

"ARTICLE 3. In part consideration of the foregoing cession, the United States do hereby set apart for the future occupancy and home of the Dakota Indians, parties to this treaty, to be held by them as Indian lands are held, all that tract of country on either side of the Minnesota River, from the western boundary of the lands herein ceded, east to the Tchay-tam-bay River [Hawk Creek in western Renville County] on the north, and to Yellow Medicine River on the south side, to extend, on each side, a distance of not less than ten miles from the general course of said river; the boundaries of said tract to be marked out as straight lines as practicable, whenever deemed expedient by the President, and in such manner as he shall direct:" which article has been stricken out of the treaty by the Senate, the said payment to be in lieu of said reservation: the amount when ascertained under instructions from the Department of the Interior, to be added to the trust-fund provided for in the fourth article.

2d. It is further stipulated, that the President be authorized, with the assent of the said band of Indians, parties to this treaty, and as soon after they shall have given their assent to the foregoing *article*, as may be convenient, to cause to be set apart by appropriate landmarks and boundaries, such tracts of country without the limits of he cession made by the first [2d] article of the treaty as may be satisfactory for their future occupancy and home: *Provided,* That the President may, by the consent of these Indians, vary the conditions aforesaid if deemed expedient.

(Treaty copied verbatim from Charles J. Kappler, editor and compiler, *Indian Affairs: Laws and Treaties* [Washington: Government Printing Office, 1904], vol. 2, pp. 588–90. Bracketed information in text of treaty added by the author.)

PART 9

Reference Notes

[1] For detailed coverage of the Manifest Destiny movement, see Albert Katz Weinberg, *Manifest Destiny: A Study of Nationalist Expansionism in American History* (Baltimore: The Johns Hopkins Press, 1935).

[2] Here and the two paragraphs below, see Arrell Morgan Gibson, *The American Indian: Prehistory to the Present* (Lexington, Mass.: D. C. Heath & Co., 1980), 188, 234, 237, 261 and Francis Paul Prucha, *The Great Father: The United States Government and the American Indians* (Lincoln: University of Nebraska Press, 1984), 14–17, 30.

[3] Gibson, *American Indian*, 269; Prucha, *Great Father*, 28–30.

[4] Prucha, *Great Father*, 50–51; U.S. Constitution, art. 1, sec. 7, 8, 10; art. 2, sec. 2.

[5] For details on the American acquisition of Minnesota, see William E. Lass, *Minnesota's Boundary with Canada: Its Evolution since 1783* (St. Paul: Minnesota Historical Society Press), 1980.

[6] William E. Lass, *Minnesota: A History* (2d ed.; New York: W. W. Norton, 1998), 82.

[7] Roy W. Meyer, *History of the Santee Sioux: United States Indian Policy on Trial* (Lincoln: University of Nebraska Press, 1967), 27.

[8] Charles J. Kappler, compiler and editor, *Indian Affairs: Laws and Treaties*, vol. 2, (Washington: Government Printing Office, 1904), 1031.

[9] *Ibid.*, William Watts Folwell, *A History of Minnesota*, vol. 1 (St. Paul: Minnesota Historical Society, 1921), 92–94.

[10] Lass, *Minnesota's Boundary with Canada*, 31–32.

[11] Kappler, *Indian Affairs*, 2: 111–23.

[12] *Ibid.*, 2: 113.

[13] June Drenning Holmquist and Jean A. Brookins, *Minnesota's Major Historic Sites: A Guide* (St. Paul: Minnesota Historical Society, 1972), 1–3.

[14] Meyer, *Santee Sioux*, 34–35.

[15] "The Northwest Ordinance," in Henry Steele Commager, *Documents of American History*, vol. 1 (7th ed.; New York: Appleton-Century-Crofts, 1963), 128–32.

[16] Kappler, *Indian Laws*, 2:250-55.

[17] Here and the paragraph below [Lawrence Taliaferro], "Auto-Biography of Maj. Lawrence Taliaferro," *Collections of the Minnesota Historical Society*, vol. 6 (St. Paul, 1894), 203–06.

[18] Jerome O. Steffen, "Clark William" and Joel H. Sibley, "Cass, Lewis," both in *American National Biography*, vol. 4 (New York: Oxford University Press, 1999), 546–47, 953–55.

[19] Here and the paragraph below Kappler, *Indian Affairs,* 2: 250-52.

[20] Here and the two paragraphs below Kappler, Indian Affairs, 305–10; Leland L. Sage, *A History of Iowa* (Ames: Iowa State University Press, 1974), 47.

[21] Kappler, Indian Treaties, 2: 307; Folwell, *History*, 1: 158.

[22] Meyer, *Santee Sioux*, 55–57.

[23] Here and the paragraph below Kappler, *Indian Affairs,* 2: 493–94.

[24] *Ibid.*, 491–93.

[25] For a summary of this national expansion, see Ray Allen Billington, *Westward Expansion: A History of the American Frontier* (4th ed.; New York: Macmillan Publishing Co., 1974). Chaps. 22, 23 and 26.

[26] Division of Wisconsin and Establishment of Iowa Territory Act, *U.S. Statutes at Large 5*: 235 (1838).

[27] For a detailed consideration of this thinking, see William E. Lass, "Minnesota's Separation from Wisconsin: Boundary Making on the Upper Mississippi Frontier," *Minnesota History* 50: 309–20 (Winter 1987).

[28] Lass, *Minnesota*, (1998), 97–101; Folwell, *Minnesota,* 1: 222–24. St. Anthony, which was merged with Minneapolis in 1872 by an act of the Minnesota legislature, consisted of that part of present-day Minneapolis east of the Mississippi River. (Warren Upham, *Minnesota Geographic Names: Their Origin and Historic Significance*, St. Paul: Minnesota Historical Society, 1920), 223.

[29] Lass, "Minnesota's Separation," 309–10, 320.

[30] For the involved maneuvering that led to the creation of Minnesota Territory, see William E. Lass, "The Birth of Minnesota," *Minnesota History* 55: 267–79 (Summer 1997).

[31] Here and the paragraph below Folwell, *Minnesota,* 1: 243–48.

[32] Minnesota Territory, *Council Journal,* 1849, 8; Folwell, *History,* 1: 352.

[33] Rhoda R. Gilman, *Henry Hastings Sibley: Divided Heart* (St. Paul: Minnesota Historical Society Press, 2004), 117–18.

[34] Here and the paragraph below, *Ibid.,* 47–50; Rhoda R. Gilman, "Last Days of the Upper Mississippi Fur Trade," *Minnesota History* 42: 122–40 (Winter 1970).

[35] Sibley to Pierre Chouteau, Jr., and Company, November 3, 1850, in Henry Hastings Sibley Papers. Microfilm copy in Memorial Library, Minnesota State University, Mankato. Originals in Minnesota Historical Society, St. Paul.

[36] Folwell, *Minnesota,* 1: 266–70; *Statistical View of the United States…Being a Compendium of the Seventh Census* (Washington: Beverly Tucker, Senate Printer, 1854), 45, 63, 82.

[37] John D. Unruh, Jr., *The Plains Across: The Overland Emigrants and the Trans-Mississippi West, 1840–60* (Urbana: University of Illinois Press, 1979), 120; On Minnesota promotion, see William E. Lass, "The Eden of the West," *Minnesota History* 56: 202–24 (Winter 1998–99).

[38] Mary Wheelhouse Berthel, *Horns of Thunder: The Life and Times of James M. Goodhue Including Selections from His Writings* (St. Paul: Minnesota Historical Society, 1948), 178; Thomas Hughes, "History of Steamboating on the Minnesota River," *Collections of the Minnesota Historical Society*, vol. 10, pt. 1 (St. Paul, 1905), 134.

[39] *Minnesota Pioneer* (St. Paul), July 4, 1850.

[40] Here and the paragraph below, Hughes, "History of Steamboating," 135.

[41] *Ibid.*, 136; *Minnesota Pioneer*, August 1, 1850.

[42] *Minnesota Pioneer*, August 1, 1850.

[43] Joseph D. Chlebecek, "The Fur Trade in the Minnesota River Valley" (unp. Master's thesis; Mankato, Minn.: Mankato State University, 1997), 207, 215–15; Gilman, *Sibley*, 118.

[44] Gilman, *Sibley*, 119–21; Prucha, *Great Father*, 1: 319–22.

[45] Here and the paragraph below, Robert A. Trennert, Jr., *Indian Traders on the Middle Border: The House of Ewing, 1827–54* (Lincoln: University of Nebraska Press, 1981), 158–59; Folwell, *Minnesota* , 1: 276–77; Indian Appropriation Act, *U.S. Statutes at Large* 9: 586 (1851).

[46] Gilman, *Sibley*, 121; Richard W. Phillips, "United States Indian Policy and the Treaty of Traverse des Sioux,: A Curricular Guide" (unp. specialist thesis; Mankato, Minn.: Mankato State University, 1976), 29–30.

[47] Meyer, *Santee Sioux*, 78; W[illiam] G. Le Duc, *Minnesota Year Book for 1852* (St. Paul: W. G. Le Duc, 1852), 24.

[48] Here and the paragraph below, Le Duc, *Minnesota Year Book*, 24–26.

[49] *Minnesota Pioneer* , June 26, 1851; Le Duc, *Minnesota Year Book*, 26, 35.

[50] Le Duc, *Minnesota Year Book*, 42.

[51] Thomas Hughes, *Old Traverse des Sioux* (St. Peter, Minn.: Herald Publishing Co.,1929; reprint, St. Peter: Nicollet County Historical Society, 1993), 21, 106, 108, 109 and 114, 141. (Page numbers are to the reprint edition.)

[52] Here and the two paragraphs below Le Duc, *Minnesota Year Book*, 25–29; *Minnesota Pioneer*, July 10, 17, 1851.

[53] Le Duc, *Minnesota Year Book*, 33.

[54] *Ibid.*, 32.

[55] Here and the paragraph below, *Ibid.*, 25, 31, 44.

[56] Here and the paragraph below, *Ibid.*, 28, 36; *Minnesota Pioneer*, July 10, 17, 1851.

[57] Le Duc, *Minnesota Year Book*, 38.

[58] *Ibid.*, 29–30.

[59] Le Duc, *Minnesota Year Book*, 62; [Mayer, Frank Blackwell], *With Pen and Pencil on the Frontier in 1851: The Diary and Sketches of Frank Blackwell Mayer*, edited with an Introduction and Notes by Bertha L. Heilbron (St. Paul: Minnesota Historical Society, 1932), 199. Also see William E. Lass, "Report on Research About Treaty of Traverse des Sioux Historic Site," (August 2000), 10–11. Copy in Treaty Site History Center. Lass prepared the report in response to a request from the

Minnesota Historical Society and the Nicollet County Historical Society. He concluded that the treaty arbor was at the site marked by the boulder with an engraved plate. But, he also determined that the boulder was not present in 1851 and hence the treaty rock tradition was false.

[60] Le Duc, *Minnesota Year Book*, 52.

[61] *Ibid.*, 43.

[62] Stuart to Lea and Ramsey, May 16, 1851, Alexander Ramsey Papers, microfilm copy in Memorial Library, Minnesota State University, Mankato, originals in Minnesota Historical Society, St. Paul.

[63] Le Duc, *Minnesota Year Book*, 43.

[64] *Ibid.*, 54.

[65] *Ibid.*, 55.

[66] *Ibid.*, 56–57.

[67] *Ibid.*, 58.

[68] Here and the paragraph below *Ibid.*, 58–59.

[69] *Ibid.*, 60.

[70] *Ibid.*, 61.

[71] Here and the paragraph below, *Minnesota Pioneer*, August 7, 1851.

[72] *Ibid.*, Typescript of Mayer's diary, in Frank Blackwell Mayer Papers, Minnesota Historical Society, St. Paul; Bertha L Heilbron, "Frank B. Mayer and the Treaties of 1851," *Minnesota History 22* (June 1941): 143.

[73] *Minnesota Pioneer*, August 7, 1851.

[74] Le Duc, *Minnesota Year Book*, 66.

[75] *Minnesota Pioneer*, August 7, 1851.

[76] *Ibid.*

[77] Folwell, *Minnesota*, 1: 282–83; For a verbatim copy of the traders' paper, see *Report of the Secretary of the Interior Communicating Further Information in Relation to the Allegations of Fraud by Alexander Ramsey*, 32 Cong., 2 sess., Senate Executive Document 29, pt. 2 (Serial 660), 22–24.

[78] Lass, "Report on Research," 11.

[79] *Minnesota Pioneer*, August 7, 1851.

[80] For a description of the Mendota negotiations, see Meyer, *Santee Sioux*, 81–84. See Kappler, *Indian Affairs*, 2:591-93 for a verbatim copy of the treaty.

[81] Stuart to Lea and Ramsey, May 16, 1851, Ramsey Papers; Ella Hawkinson, "The Old Crossing Chippewa Treaty and Its Sequel," *Minnesota History* 15: 283 (September 1934).

[82] Ibid. ; For a verbatim copy of the treaty, see Vine Deloria, Jr. and Raymond J. DeMallie, *Documents of American Indian Diplomacy: Treaties, Agreements, and Conventions, 1775–1979* (Norman: University of Oklahoma Press, 1999). 2: 798–801.

[83] Kappler, *Indian Affairs*, 2: 591. Thomas Hughes reported the combined cessions of Traverse des Sioux and Mendota amounted to "over 19,000,000 acres in Minnesota, nearly 3,000,000 acres in Iowa, and over 1,750,000 acres in South Dakota." ("The Treaty of Traverse des Sioux in 1851 under Governor Alexander Ramsey with Notes of the Former Treaty There, in 1841,

under Governor James D. Doty, of Wisconsin," *Collections of the Minnesota Historical Society*, vol. 10, pt. 1 (St. Paul, 1905), 112.

[84] The 1851 dollar is the equivalent of $26.31 in 2010 dollars. "Consumer Price Index (Estimate) 1800–2008," Accessed 10 November 2010. To access on-line input title exactly as shown.

[85] Lucile M. Kane, "The Sioux Treaties and the Traders," *Minnesota History* 32: 66 (June 1951); Stuart to Lea and Ramsey, May 16, 1851, Ramsey Papers; An Act to Amend an Act Regarding Organization of the Indian Department, *Statutes at Large* 9:203.

[86] Kane, "Sioux Treaties," 74, 76; Trennert, *Indian Traders*, 158; Le Duc, *Minnesota Year Book*, 26.

[87] Here and the two paragraphs below, *Report of the Secretary of the Interior*, 25–36; Kane, "Sioux Treaties," 76–79; Folwell, *Minnesota*, 1: 283–84, 289–90.

[88] Here and the two paragraphs below, *Journal of the Executive Proceedings of the Senate*, 32 Cong.,1 sess., 368, 376, 380–84, 391.

[89] *Ibid.*, 391, 397–98; Folwell, *Minnesota*, 1: 290. Conceptualizing North and South as they were in 1852 is not as easy as one might assume. North and South are oftentimes thought of as being divided by the Mason-Dixon line (i.e. the Maryland-Pennsylvania boundary). This definition would mean that in 1852 sixteen of the thirty-one states were free (i.e. slavery was banned) and fifteen were slave (i.e. slavery was legal). However, only eleven of the slave states later joined the Confederate States of America. Thus, the South of 1861–65 did not include the former slave states of

Delaware, Kentucky, Maryland and Missouri. (T. Harry Williams, Richard N. Current and Frank Freidel, *A History of the United States [to 1876]* (New York: Alfred A. Knopf, 1959), 509, 563.)

[90] *Executive Proceedings of the Senate*, 397.

[91] Kappler, *Indian Affairs*, 2:590.

[92] *Executive Proceedings of the Senate*, 398.

[93] Here and the paragraph below, *Executive Proceedings of the Senate*, 401, 405.

[94] Meyer, *Santee Sioux*, 86; Gilman, Sibley, 131.

[95] Here and the paragraph below Folwell, *Minnesota*, 1:293–94; Gilman, *Sibley*, 131–32: Kappler, *Indian Affairs*, 2: 588. Technically, the president's proclamation was the ratification of a treaty. Numerous observers including many contemporaries to the treaties refer to the Senate ratifying treaties. But the constitution does not stipulate that the Senate ratify treaties, but rather that it give its "advice and consent". Therefore with respect to treaties, ratification is an executive rather than a legislative action. (U.S. Constitution, art. 2, sec. 2.)

[96] Meyer, *Santee Sioux*, 84.

[97] George E. Warner and Charles M. Foote, eds., *History of the Minnesota Valley*...(Minneapolis: North Star Publishing Co.), 297, 411, 480, 638: Thomas Hughes, *History of Blue Earth County* (Chicago: Middle West Publishing Co., [1909]), 34–36; *Henderson Then and Now* (Henderson: City of Henderson, 1995), 41–42.

[98] Lass, *Minnesota*, 112.

[99] Here and the paragraph below. Meyer, *Santee Sioux*, 89–90.

[100] Here and the paragraph below, Folwell, *Minnesota*, 1: 247 ,360.

[101] For an excellent summary of reservation life, see Meyer, *Santee Sioux*, chap. 5.

[102] For a concise, objective history of the Dakota War see Kenneth Carley, *The Sioux Uprising of 1862* (2d ed.; St. Paul: Minnesota Historical Society, 1976. In 2001 the society reprinted this book under the title *The Dakota War of 1862*.

[103] Relief of Persons for Damages Caused by Depredations of Sioux Indians Act and Removal of Dakota Indians and Disposition of Their Lands Act, *U.S. Statutes at Large*, 12:652–54, 819–20 (1863).

[104] William E. Lass, "The Removal from Minnesota of the Sioux and Winnebago Indians," *Minnesota History* 38 (December 1963): 353–64; Meyer, *Santee Sioux*, 137.

[105] Roy W. Meyer, "The Canadian Sioux: Refugees from Minnesota," *Minnesota History 41* (Spring 1968): 13–28.

[106] Kappler, *Indian Affairs*, 2: 956–59.

[107] [Mayer], *With Pen and Pencil*, 17–19; Robert L. Gale, "Millet, Francis Davis," *American National Biography*, Vol. 15 (New York: Oxford University Press, 1999), 525–27. Millet's eventful life was ended when the passenger ship *Titanic* sank in the North Atlantic on April 15, 1912.

[108] Paul Little, *Dakota Perspective on Traverse des Sioux Nicollet County, Minnesota* ([St. Paul]: Archaeology Department, Minnesota Historical Society, 1995), 1.

[109] As quoted in Folwell, *Minnesota,* 1: 304.

[110] Jack Utter, *American Indians: Answers to Today's Questions,* (2d ed.; Norman: University of Oklahoma Press, 2001), 86.

Part 10
Bibliography

Articles:

Gale, Robert L. "Millet, Francis Davis." *American National Biography*, vol. 15. New York: Oxford University Press, 1999.

Gilman, Rhoda R. "Last Days of the Upper Mississippi Fur Trade." *Minnesota History* 42 (Winter 1970): 122–40.

Hawkinson, Ella. "The Old Crossing Chippewa Treaty and Its Sequel." *Minnesota History* 15 (September 1934): 282–300.

Heilbron, Bertha L. "Frank B. Mayer and the Treaties of 1851." *Minnesota History* 22 (June 1941): 133–56.

Hughes, Thomas. "History of Steamboating on the Minnesota River." *Collections of the Minnesota Historical Society*, vol. 10, pt. 1: 131–63. St. Paul, 1905.

______. "The Treaty of Traverse des Sioux in 1851, under Governor Alexander Ramsey, with Notes of the Former Treaty There, in 1841, under James D. Doty, of Wisconsin." *Collections of the Minnesota Historical Society*, vol. 10, pt. 1: 100–29. St. Paul, 1905.

Kane, Lucile M. "The Sioux Treaties and the Traders." *Minnesota History* 32 (June 1951): 65–80.

Lass, William E. "The Birth of Minnesota." *Minnesota History* 55 (Summer 1997): 267–79.

_______. "The Eden of the West." *Minnesota History* 56 (Winter 1998–99): 202–24.

_______. "Minnesota's Separation from Wisconsin: Boundary Making on the Upper Mississippi Frontier." *Minnesota History* 50 (Winter 1987): 309–20.

_______. "The Removal from Minnesota of the Sioux and Winnebago Indians." *Minnesota History* 38 (December 1963): 353–64.

Meyer, Roy W. "The Canadian Sioux: Refugees from Minnesota." *Minnesota History* 41 (Spring 1968): 13–28.

Sibley, Joel H. "Cass, Lewis." *American National Biography*, vol. 4. New York: Oxford University Press, 1999.

Steffen, Jerome O. "Clark, William." *American National Biography*, vol. 4. New York: Oxford University Press, 1999.

[Taliaferro, Lawrence]. "Auto-Biography of Maj. Lawrence Taliaferro. *Collections of the Minnesota Historical Society*, vol. 6: 189–255. St. Paul, 1894.

Books:

Berthel, Mary Wheelhouse. *Horns of Thunder: The Life and Times of James M. Goodhue Including Selections from His Writings*. St. Paul: Minnesota Historical Society, 1948.

Billington, Ray Allen. *Westward Expansion: A History of the American Frontier*. 4th ed. New York: Macmillan Publishing Co., 1974.

Carley, Kenneth. *The Sioux Uprising of 1862*. 2d ed. St. Paul: Minnesota Historical Society, 1976.

Commager, Henry Steele. *Documents of American History*, vol. 1. 7th ed. New York: Appleton-Century-Crofts, 1963.

Deloria, Vine, Jr. and Raymond J. DeMallie, *Documents of American Indian Diplomacy: Treaties, Agreements, and Conventions,1775–1979*. Norman: University of Oklahoma Press, 1999.

Folwell, William Watts. *A History of Minnesota*, vol. 1. St. Paul: Minnesota Historical Society, 1921.

Gibson, Arrell Morgan. *The American Indian: Prehistory to the Present*. Lexington, Mass.: D.C. Heath & Co., 1980.

Gilman, Rhoda R. *Henry Hastings Sibley: Divided Heart*. St. Paul: Minnesota Historical Society Press, 2004.

Henderson Then and Now. Henderson, Minn.: City of Henderson, 1995.

Holmquist, June Drenning and Jean A. Brookins. *Minnesota's Major Historic Sites: A Guide*. St. Paul: Minnesota Historical Society, 1972.

Hughes, Thomas. *History of Blue Earth County*. Chicago: Middle West Publishing Co., [1909].

_______. *Old Traverse des Sioux*. St. Peter, Minn.: Herald Publishing Co.,1929. Reprint, St. Peter: Nicollet County Historical Society, 1993.

Kappler, Charles J., compiler and editor. *Indian Affairs: Laws and Treaties*, vol. 2. Washington: Government Printing Office, 1904.

Lass, William E. *Minnesota: A History*. 2d ed. New York: W. W. Norton, 1998.

_______. *Minnesota's Boundary with Canada: Its Evolution since 1783*. St. Paul: Minnesota Historical Society Press, 1980.

Le Duc, W[illiam] G. *Minnesota Year Book for 1852*. St. Paul: W. G. Le Duc, 1852.

[Mayer, Frank Blackwell]. *With Pen and Pencil on the Frontier in 1851: The Diary and Sketches of Frank Blackwell Mayer*. Edited with an Introduction and Notes by Bertha L. Heilbron. St. Paul: Minnesota Historical Society, 1932.

Meyer, Roy W. *History of the Santee Sioux: United States Indian Policy on Trial*. Lincoln: University of Nebraska Press, 1967.

Prucha, Francis Paul. *The Great Father: The United States Government and the American Indians*. Lincoln: University of Nebraska Press, 1984.

Sage, Leland L. *A History of Iowa*. Ames: Iowa State University Press, 1974.

Trennert, Robert A., Jr. *Indian Traders on the Middle Border: The House of Ewing, 1827–54*. Lincoln: University of Nebraska Press, 1981.

Unruh, John D., Jr. *The Plains Across: The Overland Emigrants and the Trans-Mississippi West, 1840–60*. Urbana: University of Illinois Press, 1979.

Upham, Warren. *Minnesota Geographic Names: Their Origin and Historic Significance.* St. Paul: Minnesota Historical Society, 1920.

Utter, Jack. *American Indians: Answers to Today's Questions.* 2d ed. Norman: University of Oklahoma Press, 2001.

Warner, George E. and Charles M. Foote, eds. *History of the Minnesota Valley....* Minneapolis: North Star Publishing Co., 1881.

Weinberg, Albert Katz. *Manifest Destiny: A Study of Nationalist Expansion in American History.* Baltimore: The Johns Hopkins Press, 1935.

Williams, T. Harry, Richard N. Current and Frank Freidel. *A History of the United States [to 1876].* New York: Alfred A. Knopf, 1959.

Government documents and publications:

Journal of the Executive Proceedings of the Senate. 32 Cong., 1 sess. (1852).

Minnesota Territory. *Council Journal,* 1849.

Report of the Secretary of the Interior Communicating Further Information in Relation to the Allegations of Fraud by Alexander Ramsey. 32 Cong., 2 sess., Senate Executive Document 29, pt. 2 (Serial 660).

Statistical View of the United States...Being a Compendium of the Seventh Census. Washington: Beverly Tucker, Senate Printer, 1854.

U.S. Constitution.

U.S. An Act to Amend an Act Regarding Organization of the Indian Department. *Statutes at Large 9* (1847).

U.S. Division of Wisconsin Territory and Establishment of Iowa Territory Act. *Statutes at Large 5* (1838).

U.S. Indian Appropriation Act. *Statutes at Large 9* (1851).

U.S. Removal of Dakota Indians and Disposition of Their Lands Act. *Statutes at Large 12* (1863).

Manuscripts:

Mayer, Frank Blackwell. Papers. Minnesota Historical Society, St. Paul.

Ramsey, Alexander. Papers. Microfilm copy in Memorial Library, Minnesota State University, Mankato. Originals in Minnesota Historical Society, St. Paul.

Sibley, Henry Hastings. Papers. Microfilm copy in Memorial Library, Minnesota State University, Mankato. Originals in Minnesota Historical Society, St. Paul.

Newspaper:

Minnesota Pioneer (St. Paul), June–August, 1851.

Other:

Chlebecek, Joseph D. "The Fur Trade in the Minnesota River Valley." Unp. Master's thesis. Mankato State University, Mankato Minn., 1997.

"Consumer Price Index (Estimate) 1800–2008." On-line source. To access input title exactly as shown.

Lass, William E. "Report on Research About Treaty of Traverse des Sioux Historic Site." August, 2000. Copy in Treaty Site History Center, St. Peter, Minn.

Little, Paul. *Dakota Perspective on Traverse des Sioux, Nicollet County, Minnesota*. [St. Paul]: Archaeology Department, Minnesota Historical Society.1995.

Phillips, Richard W. "United States Indian Policy and the Treaty of Traverse des Sioux: A Curricular Guide." Unp. specialist thesis. Mankato State University, 1976.